SEVEN WONDERS OF PRESERVATION

Seven Wonders of Preservation

UNESCO's World Heritage

RAFEAL MECHLORE

PREACH PUBLICATIONS

CONTENTS

Table of Contents

4.1 Detailed explanation of the nomination and inscription process.

4.2 The role of advisory bodies and site management.

4.3 How communities and countries benefit from World Heritage status.

Chapter 5:Challenges and Threats

5.1 Examination of common threats to World Heritage Sites:

5.2 Climate change.

5.3 Tourism pressures.

5.4 Armed conflict and vandalism.

5.5 Case studies illustrating these challenges.

Chapter 6:Preservation Success Stories

6.1 Inspiring stories of successful preservation and restoration efforts:

6.2 The restoration of Venice and its lagoon, Italy.

6.3 The recovery of Angkor Wat, Cambodia.

6.4 The revitalization of the Historic Center of Oaxaca, Mexico.

6.5 The importance of community involvement.

Chapter 7:Beyond the Wonders: Cultural Exchange

7.1 The role of World Heritage Sites in fostering global cultural exchange.

7.2 Examples of international collaborations and partnerships.

7.3 The cultural and economic impact of tourism.

Chapter 8:Looking to the Future

8.1 Emerging challenges in the preservation of world heritage.

8.2 Innovations and technologies aiding conservation efforts.

8.3 The evolving role of UNESCO in the 21st century.

Chapter 9:Conclusion

9.1 Recap of the significance of UNESCO's World Heritage program.

9.2 The responsibility of current and future generations in preservation.

9.3 Final thoughts on the enduring importance of the seven wonders of preservation.

Introduction

Seven Miracles of Protection: UNESCO's Reality Legacy

In the tremendous embroidery of mankind's set of experiences, certain strings stick out, woven with strings of imaginativeness, regular magnificence, and the unyielding entry of time. These strings are our legacy, heritages from an earlier time that span the gap between what and is. From the transcending pyramids of Egypt to the delicate environments of the Galápagos Islands, these fortunes recount accounts of human inventiveness, the getting through influence of nature, and the aggregate goals of our world-wide development. They are, basically, the Seven Miracles of Safe-guarding — the point of convergence of this investigation into the core of UNESCO's Reality Legacy program.

The World Legacy program, laid out by the Unified Countries Instructive, Logical and Social Association (UNESCO) in 1972, has turned into an image of global collaboration and a demonstration of our obligation to protecting the indispensable. It addresses an aggregate vow to safeguard and save the world's most extraordinary social and normal destinations for people in the future. As we set out on this excursion to reveal the complexities and meaning of these fortunes, we'll observe that they are something beyond puts on a rundown. They are living demonstrations of our common human story, our interweaved relationship with the climate, and our obligation as stewards of the Earth.

The Introduction of World Legacy

To comprehend the World Legacy program and the marvels it looks to secure, we should first rewind the verifiable embroidery to when the world was grappling with the significant effect of industrialization, urbanization, and the quick speed of advancement. During the twentieth 100 years, these powers were reshaping the physical and social scenes of our planet at an extraordinary speed. Antiquated urban areas disintegrated under the heaviness of modernization, and delicate biological systems wilted under the tireless walk of progress.

Amidst this change, the world's social and normal legacy remained in danger. UNESCO, made in 1945 with the mission of advancing harmony and collaboration through training, science, and culture, perceived the direness of the circumstance. They comprehended that the deficiency of these exceptional locales would be an unsalvageable misfortune to mankind. This acknowledgment prompted the introduction of the World Legacy program.

On November 16, 1972, the Overall Meeting of UNESCO took on the World Legacy Show, a global arrangement pointed toward distinguishing and protecting locales of remarkable worth. The Show was imaginative in its methodology, presenting the idea of "general worth" and "remarkable widespread importance."

This implied that the chose locales shouldn't just be of significance to the country in which they were found yet in addition hold importance for all of mankind. This weighty thought established the groundwork for what might become one of the most regarded and viable legacy protection drives on the planet.

With the Show's reception, UNESCO left on the errand of distinguishing and writing the principal World Legacy Destinations — places that would represent the responsibility of countries to save and safeguard their common legacy. In 1978, the primary rundown of World Legacy Destinations was distributed, highlighting a blend of regular miracles and social wonders, from Yellowstone Public Park in the US to the noteworthy focus of Quito, Ecuador.

These debut locales set up for a worldwide undertaking to protect our legacy. Today, the World Legacy Rundown incorporates north of 1,000 destinations spread across in excess of 160 nations, each a demonstration of the rich variety of human societies and the surprising excellence of our normal world. On the whole, they recount to a story that rises above boundaries and ages, a story that addresses the substance of being human.

Social Legacy Marvels

Our investigation of the Seven Marvels of Safeguarding starts with an excursion into the domain of social legacy. These are the locales that demonstrate the veracity of the accomplishments of our precursors, the works of art of design and imaginativeness that have formed the course of development. They are the extensions that associate us to our past, the reverberations of voices a distant memory, and the living articulations of human inventiveness.

The Pyramids of Giza, Egypt

The Pyramids of Giza, rising grandly from the parched sands of Egypt, are among the most famous and persevering through images of human accomplishment. Constructed over four centuries prior, these fantastic burial chambers filled in as the last resting places for Pharaohs and have caught the creative mind of individuals overall for a really long time. The Incomparable Pyramid of Giza, otherwise called the Pyramid of Khufu, remains as the last overcomer of the first Seven Miracles of the Antiquated World.

As we dive into the structural wonder of the Pyramids, we will reveal the privileged insights of their development, the numerical accuracy utilized by old Egyptians, and the getting through secret of how they accomplished such accomplishments with the innovation of their time. We will likewise investigate the difficulties of saving these antiquated miracles even with present day pressures and the significance of social legacy in forming contemporary character.

The Incomparable Mass of China

Extending like a twisted mythical beast across the immense scenes of China, the Incomparable Wall isn't simply an actual obstruction however an image of China's rich history and versatility. It is a demonstration of human assurance and the courage of old civilizations.

Initially built to safeguard China from intrusions, this titanic design winds through mountains, deserts, and fields, making a permanent imprint on the scene.

Our investigation of the Incomparable Wall will take us on an excursion through its set of experiences, from its beginnings in the seventh century BC to its development during the Ming Tradition. We will find out about the wall's essential importance, its social imagery, and the difficulties it faces in the advanced period, as segments of it disintegrate under the heaviness of time and the travel industry.

Machu Picchu, Peru

High in the Andes Heaps of Peru lies Machu Picchu, an Incan bastion covered in fog and secret. This old city, roosted on an edge between two transcending tops, was inherent the fifteenth hundred years and later deserted. Failed to remember by the rest of the world for a really long time, it was rediscovered in 1911 by American student of history and pioneer Hiram Bingham.

Machu Picchu's dazzling engineering, multifaceted stone workmanship, and amazing normal setting make it quite possibly of the most notorious archeological site on earth. Our excursion to this site will reveal its importance as a demonstration of the designing ability of the Inca civilization and the difficulties looked in protecting its sensitive designs in the midst of a developing convergence of travelers.

The Acropolis of Athens, Greece

The Acropolis of Athens, delegated by the Parthenon, remains as an image of old Greece's commitments to craftsmanship, reasoning, and a majority rule government. Roosted on a rough slope sitting above the city of Athens, the Acropolis is a magnum opus of old style Greek design and a demonstration of the getting through tradition of Western civilization.

As we investigate the Acropolis, we will dig into the historical backdrop of old Greece, the meaning of the Parthenon as a sanctuary to Athena, and the difficulties of saving its marble segments and models notwithstanding contamination and time's determined walk.

These four social marvels address the apex of human accomplishment, exhibiting the resourcefulness and innovativeness of civic establishments long past. In any case, their safeguarding isn't without its hardships, from the impacts of environmental change to the tensions of mass the travel industry. In the pages that follow, we will travel through the difficulties and accomplishments of safeguarding these social fortunes, figuring out how they keep on rousing stunningness and love in the cutting edge world.

Normal Legacy Miracles

Past the domain of human imaginativeness, the miracles of the normal world allure us to investigate and wonder about the magnificence and variety of our planet.

From unblemished environments to striking scenes, these regular legacy ponders help us to remember our profound association with the Earth and the critical need to safeguard it.

The Galápagos Islands, Ecuador

Distant the shore of Ecuador, the Galápagos Islands are a residing research center of development, where Charles Darwin's experiences into regular determination were conceived. These far off volcanic islands are home to a staggering cluster of animal groups found no place else on The planet, from goliath turtles to blue-footed boobies.

Our excursion to the Galápagos will bring us into the core of this extraordinary biological system, where we'll find the sensitive equilibrium that supports life on these islands and the preservation endeavors expected to safeguard it. We'll likewise investigate the difficulties presented by obtrusive species, environmental change, and human effect.

Serengeti Public Park, Tanzania

The Serengeti is an immense savannah that stretches across Tanzania and Kenya, home to one of the most fabulous natural life relocations in the world. Every year, a large number of wildebeest, zebras, and different creatures navigate this flawless scene looking for greener fields, making a stunning exhibition that has caught the minds of natural life fans and moderates the same.

As we adventure into the Serengeti, we'll observer the circle of life in real life, from the hunter prey elements to the introduction of new ages. We'll likewise dig into the protection endeavors pointed toward saving this normal miracle and the difficulties presented by environment misfortune and poaching.

Yellowstone Public Park, USA

Yellowstone, settled in the core of the American West, is a geo-thermal wonderland. Its percolating underground aquifers, danger-ous fountains, and energetic scenes make it a living demonstration of the World's land processes. It was the world's most memorable public park, a model for protection endeavors around the world.

Our investigation of Yellowstone will take us through the rec-reation area's geothermal elements, its rich biodiversity, and its social importance to Local American clans. We'll likewise look at the difficulties presented by expanded appearance, environmental change, and the sensitive harmony among human and regular bio-logical systems.

The Incomparable Obstruction Reef, Australia

Underneath the purplish blue waters of the Coral Ocean lies the Incomparable Hindrance Reef, a work of art of marine biodiversity. This rambling coral reef framework is home to a surprising assort-ment of marine life, from beautiful coral developments to subtle ocean animals. It isn't just a characteristic marvel yet additionally a basic piece of the worldwide environment.

Our excursion to the Incomparable Hindrance Reef will lower us into the universe of coral reefs, their significance to marine life, and the dangers they face from coral blanching, contamination, and sea fermentation. We'll investigate the endeavors to secure and save this submerged fortune for people in the future.

These four normal legacy ponders grandstand the mind blowing variety and flexibility of our planet's environments. They help us to remember the interconnectedness of all life and the imperative significance of protection endeavors despite mounting natural difficulties. As we dig into their accounts, we'll uncover the sensitive harmony between human exercises and the protection of these normal miracles.

The UNESCO World Legacy Cycle

At the core of the World Legacy program lies a thorough and co-operative interaction for distinguishing, selecting, and saving these remarkable destinations. An interaction includes nations, specialists, and networks from around the world, all cooperating to satisfy a common obligation to safeguard our worldwide legacy.

In the accompanying parts, we will investigate the inward operations of this cycle. We will figure out how locales are selected, assessed, and engraved on the World Legacy Rundown. We will find the job of warning bodies, like the Worldwide Gathering on Landmarks and Locales (ICOMOS) and the Global Association for Protection of Nature (IUCN), in surveying the social and normal upsides of these destinations. We will likewise dive into the obligations of site directors and nearby networks in guaranteeing the continuous security and manageability of World Legacy Destinations.

Be that as it may, the World Legacy process isn't only a regulatory activity. It is a demonstration of the force of global participation and the acknowledgment that our social and regular legacy knows no boundaries. These destinations have a place with all of mankind, and their safeguarding requires an aggregate exertion that rises above legislative issues and public interests.

As we venture further into the complexities of the World Legacy process, we will acquire a significant appreciation for the devotion of people and associations overall who work vigorously to guarantee that these fortunes persevere for a long time into the future.

Difficulties and Dangers

While the World Legacy program has accomplished huge triumphs in safeguarding our common legacy, it likewise faces a large number of difficulties and dangers. In a consistently impacting world, where environmental change, the travel industry pressures, and outfitted struggle can unleash ruin on these valuable locales, the requirement for cautiousness and transformation is principal.

In the sections that follow, we will go up against these difficulties head-on. We will investigate the effects of environmental change on social and normal legacy destinations, from the disintegration of old designs to the blanching of coral reefs. We will look at the sensitive harmony among the travel industry and protection, featuring contextual investigations where stuffing and unregulated appearance have negatively affected these fortunes.

We will likewise dive into the sobering truth of equipped clash and defacement, where World Legacy Locales have become blowback in clashes that length the globe. These accounts act as obvious tokens of the delicacy of our common legacy and the pressing need to safeguard it.

However, inside these difficulties, we will track down accounts of versatility and assurance. We will experience people and networks who won't allow affliction to delete their social and normal inheritances. Their accounts are encouraging signs, enlightening the way ahead even with apparently difficult chances.

Protection Examples of overcoming adversity

In the midst of the difficulties and dangers, there are accounts of win — of World Legacy Locales that have been reestablished from the edge of blankness and are currently brilliant illustrations of fruitful conservation endeavors. These accounts advise us that with commitment, advancement, and aggregate activity, we can beat even the most overwhelming difficulties.

In the parts ahead, we will travel to Venice and its tidal pond, where a coordinated work to battle rising waters and protect memorable engineering has yielded exceptional outcomes. We will go to Cambodia and witness the resurgence of Angkor Wat, when a neglected miracle of the old world. We will investigate the rejuvenation of the Noteworthy Focus of Oaxaca, Mexico, and the focal job of local area association in legacy protection.

These examples of overcoming adversity offer significant illustrations and motivation for safeguarding our common legacy. They show that with the right systems, organizations, and responsibility, we might defend these marvels at any point as well as guarantee that they keep on enhancing the existences of people in the future.

Past the Marvels: Social Trade

The World Legacy program isn't only about protecting actual locales; it is likewise about encouraging social trade and discourse among countries. World Legacy Destinations act as scaffolds of figuring out, interfacing individuals from different foundations through a common appreciation for our worldwide legacy.

In the sections to come, we will investigate the job of World Legacy Destinations in advancing social trade. We will analyze examples where countries have met up to help the protection of locales in different nations, rising above political limits for the sake of legacy preservation.

We will likewise think about the social and financial effect of the travel industry, as guests from around the world experience these miracles and add to the neighborhood networks that consideration for them.

These accounts of social trade advise us that our common legacy has the ability to join us in a world frequently separated by contrasts. They highlight the significance of saving these fortunes for their natural worth as well as for the obligations of understanding and collaboration they sustain among countries.

Planning ahead

As we stand on the edge of another time, the conservation of our reality's social and regular legacy faces developing difficulties and valuable open doors. In the last parts of this investigation, we will project our look forward, taking into account the way forward for UNESCO's Reality Legacy program.

We will stand up to arising difficulties, from the developing dangers of environmental change to the requirement for imaginative advances and strategies in legacy conservation. We will ponder the developing job of UNESCO in the 21st 100 years, investigating how this respected association can adjust to address the issues of an impacting world while staying consistent with its center mission.

Through everything, one thing stays clear: the significance of saving our common legacy has never been more noteworthy. An obligation falls upon the shoulders of current and people in the future, an obligation to safeguard the miracles that have enhanced our lives and characterized our ways of life as people.

In the pages that follow, we will leave on an excursion through existence, uncovering the tales of the Seven Marvels of Protection — the fortunes that help us to remember our common mankind, the magnificence of our normal world, and the getting through influence of human creativity. An excursion welcomes us to consider our job as stewards of the Earth and as watchmen of our common heritage. An excursion helps us that the miracles to remember the past are not only relics of history; they are living demonstrations of the goals of a worldwide human progress, a demonstration of the unyielding soul of conservation.

As we start this investigation, we welcome you to open your hearts and brains to the miracles that anticipate. They are something beyond puts on a rundown; they are the encapsulation of our aggregate memory, the epitome of our common future. They are the Seven Miracles of Protection, and their accounts are our own to find.

A. Brief overview of UNESCO and its World Heritage program.
A Concise Outline of UNESCO and Its Reality Legacy Program

In a universe of different societies, rich narratives, and regular ponders, the safeguarding of our common legacy has arisen as a fundamental worldwide concern. Perceiving the need to safeguard and commend these fortunes of human and regular history, the Assembled Countries Instructive, Logical and Social Association (UNESCO) laid out the World Legacy program in 1972. This program, frequently alluded to as UNESCO World Legacy, has since turned into a guide of global participation and an image of our obligation to defending the indispensable.

The Introduction of UNESCO

To comprehend the beginnings of UNESCO and its Reality Legacy program, we should travel back to the fallout of The Second Great War. The obliteration and death toll achieved by the conflict incited world pioneers to imagine an association that would advance harmony through instruction, science, and culture. On November 16, 1945, the Assembled Countries Gathering for the foundation of an instructive and social association met in London, prompting the introduction of UNESCO.

All along, UNESCO's central goal was clear: to fabricate the safeguards of harmony in the personalities of people through training, science, and culture. This mission was established on the conviction that cultivating common comprehension and regard for the world's social variety would assist with forestalling the flare-up of future contentions. In the years that followed, UNESCO worked vigorously to advance these standards, supporting schooling, logical examination, and social trade all over the planet.

The Making of the World Legacy Program

By the mid 1970s, the fast speed of improvement, urbanization, and industrialization had started to negatively affect our reality's social and normal legacy. Memorable destinations were disintegrating, immaculate conditions were vanishing, and old practices were blurring into lack of clarity. Perceiving the criticalness of the circumstance, UNESCO made a spearheading stride by laying out the World Legacy program.

The World Legacy program was officially brought into the world on November 16, 1972, when the Overall Gathering of UNESCO took on the World Legacy Show in Paris. This global deal was momentous in its methodology, presenting the idea of "widespread worth" and "remarkable general importance." It implied that the chose destinations shouldn't just be of significance to the country in which they were found yet additionally hold importance for all of mankind. This visionary thought established the groundwork for what might become one of the world's most eminent legacy conservation drives.

The Meaning of World Legacy Locales

World Legacy Locales, as characterized by the Show, are spots of social, normal, or blended (both social and regular) importance that are viewed as of remarkable worth to mankind. These destinations address a mosaic of the world's different legacy, incorporating everything from design wonders and noteworthy urban communities to stunning normal scenes and environments.

World Legacy Locales act as living demonstrations of the accomplishments of past developments, the excellence of the normal world, and the interchange between human culture and the climate. They are spots where history, culture, science, and protection unite, offering a significant association with our common human story and the planet we call home.

The World Legacy Rundown

The core of the World Legacy program lies On the planet Legacy Rundown — an extensive index of locales that have been recorded in light of their uncommon worth. These destinations go through a thorough designation and assessment process that includes specialists, legislatures, and the collaboration of nations around the world.

To be remembered for the World Legacy Rundown, a site should meet rigid rules, including showing its "extraordinary widespread worth" and having viable systems for security and the board. Locales are assessed by warning bodies, like the Worldwide Committee on Landmarks and Destinations (ICOMOS) for social destinations and the Global Association for Protection of Nature (IUCN) for regular destinations. A ultimate choice is made by the World Legacy Panel, made out of delegates from UNESCO part states.

Starting around my last information update in September 2021, the World Legacy Rundown highlighted north of 1,000 locales spreading over in excess of 160 nations. These destinations incorporate famous ponders like the Incomparable Mass of China, the Pyramids of Giza, the Galápagos Islands, and Yellowstone Public Park, to give some examples. Every engraving addresses a common obligation to secure and safeguard our reality's most outstanding social and regular fortunes.

The Job of the World Legacy Program

The World Legacy program assumes a complex part in the worldwide field:

Protection and Safeguarding: One of its essential capabilities is to distinguish and assign World Legacy Locales, perceiving their extraordinary widespread worth. Through this interaction, UNESCO means to guarantee the safeguarding and insurance of these locales for people in the future.

Schooling and Mindfulness: The program brings issues to light about the significance of legacy safeguarding. It teaches individuals about the meaning of these locales and their job in our common human story.

Social Trade: World Legacy Locales act as scaffolds for social trade, encouraging discourse and understanding among individuals from different foundations. They are scenes for diverse associations and appreciation.

Monetary and Reasonable Turn of events: Numerous World Legacy Destinations are crucial for neighborhood economies through the travel industry and occupation creation. The program advances economical improvement that adjusts the necessities of networks with the basic to safeguard these destinations.

Logical Exploration: The program empowers logical examination and studies connected with legacy preservation, from engineering reclamation strategies to biodiversity protection.

Crisis Reaction: UNESCO offers help in the midst of crises, like furnished clashes or cataclysmic events, to safeguard World Legacy Destinations from harm or obliteration.

The Continuous Difficulties

While UNESCO's Reality Legacy program has taken critical steps in protecting our common legacy, it faces a large group of difficulties and dangers. Environmental change, uncontrolled the travel industry, equipped clash, and political insecurity keep on endangering these valuable destinations. Adjusting the necessities of preservation with the interests of nearby networks and states can likewise be a sensitive and complex undertaking.

As the program pushes ahead, it should wrestle with the developing scene of legacy conservation. The requirement for imaginative preservation methodologies, economical the travel industry the executives, and variation to ecological changes are only a portion of the major problems that require consideration.

B.The significance of preserving cultural and natural heritage.

The Meaning of Saving Social and Regular Legacy

Our reality is an embroidery woven with strings of mankind's set of experiences, normal excellence, and social variety. Inside this perplexing texture lie the fortunes of our common legacy, both social and regular, that interface us to our past, characterize our present, and shape our future. The meaning of protecting these legacy resources couldn't possibly be more significant, as they act as a guide of grasping, a wellspring of personality, and a demonstration of the persevering through human soul.

A Living Record of Mankind's Set of experiences

Social legacy includes the unmistakable and immaterial appearances of human innovativeness and inventiveness. It is a living record of our set of experiences, mirroring the convictions, values, and accomplishments of developments over the course of time. Safeguarding social legacy guarantees that these heritages stay available to present and people in the future.

1. **Saving Our Character:** Social legacy shapes the ground-work of our personalities. It recounts the tales of our pro-genitors, their battles, wins, and the aggregate insight they passed down. Whether through antiquated ancient rarities, compositional wonders, or customary practices, social legacy associates us to our underlying foundations, assisting us with understanding where we come from.

2. **Encouraging Comprehension:** Social legacy cultivates cul-turally diverse comprehension and appreciation. By investi-gating the practices, craftsmanship, and customs of various societies, we gain bits of knowledge into the rich embroidered artwork of human variety. It advances sympathy, regard, and a feeling of shared mankind.

3. **Gaining from the Past:** Social legacy is a wellspring of infor-mation. It gives important bits of knowledge into past social orders, their developments, and their reactions to challenges. These examples from history can illuminate our choices in the present and guide us toward an additional economical and amicable future.

The Biological and Tasteful Worth of Nature

Regular legacy, then again, envelops the shocking scenes, en-vironments, and species that have developed over centuries. These regular miracles hold both environmental and stylish worth, mak-ing them fundamental to the prosperity of our planet and our own personal satisfaction.

1. **Biodiversity and Environment Administrations:** Regular legacy destinations frequently harbor extraordinary bio-diversity. These regions are home to endless species, a large number of which are found no place else on The planet. Saving these environments is fundamental for rationing bio-diversity and the biological system administrations they

give, like clean air and water, fertilization, and environment guideline.

2. **Tasteful and Persuasive Worth:** Normal legacy destinations rouse stunningness and miracle. From immaculate rainforests to transcending mountains and perfect shorelines, these scenes associate us to the excellence and magnificence of the normal world. They offer spots for amusement, profound reflection, and imaginative motivation.

3. **Social and Customary Associations:** Regular legacy is frequently interwoven with social practices and native information. Numerous people group depend on these regular assets for their livelihoods, and their conservation is fundamental for supporting these lifestyles.

Difficulties to Protection

While the meaning of saving social and regular legacy is clear, it isn't without its difficulties. Both social and regular legacy face dangers from different quarters, including:

1. **Environmental Change:** Climbing temperatures, ocean level ascent, and outrageous climate occasions represent a critical danger to both social and normal legacy. Beach front legacy locales are in danger from ocean level ascent, while biological systems and species face territory disturbance and annihilation.

2. **Unreasonable Turn of events:** Urbanization, foundation improvement, and unregulated the travel industry can prompt the corruption and annihilation of legacy locales. These exercises can dissolve the credibility and honesty of social destinations and disturb normal biological systems.

3. **Contamination and Ecological Debasement:** Contamination, like air and water contamination, adversely influences both social and regular legacy. For instance, air contamination can

prompt the decay of memorable structures and landmarks, while water contamination hurts sea-going environments.

4. **Equipped Struggle and Defacing:** Social legacy destinations are especially powerless during seasons of furnished struggle and common turmoil. Purposeful annihilation, plundering, and defacing can bring about the deficiency of indispensable social fortunes.

5. **The travel industry Tensions:** While the travel industry can carry financial advantages to neighborhood networks, uncontrolled the travel industry can put critical weight on legacy destinations. Stuffing, foundation advancement, and deficient waste administration can hurt both social and normal legacy.

The Basic of Protection

Saving our social and normal legacy isn't simply a choice; it is a basic established in moral, natural, and social contemplations. The following are a few convincing justifications for why legacy protection is imperative:

1. **Stewardship for People in the future:** We have an honest conviction to give our legacy to people in the future flawless. By safeguarding these fortunes, we guarantee that our relatives can encounter a similar miracle and appreciation for their social and normal environmental elements.

2. **Feasible Turn of events:** Legacy protection adds to practical advancement by giving financial open doors, saving conventional information, and advancing dependable the travel industry. It assists networks with flourishing while at the same time monitoring their interesting character.

3. **Environment Flexibility:** Safeguarding normal legacy locales can improve environment versatility by safeguarding biological systems that offer basic types of assistance like flood control, carbon sequestration, and water purging.

4. **Instruction and Mindfulness:** Social and normal legacy destinations are significant instructive assets. They give chances to finding out about history, nature, and the interconnectedness of people and the climate.

5. **Worldwide Participation:** Legacy conservation is a worldwide undertaking that encourages global collaboration and understanding. UNESCO's Reality Legacy program is a brilliant illustration of how countries can meet up to safeguard our common fortunes.

Abstract

The Seven Miracles of Protection epitomize the pith of UNESCO's Reality Legacy program and its getting through significance in shielding our common social and regular legacy. These marvels stand as images of social variety, human inventiveness, and the wonder of the normal world. They are a demonstration of world-wide participation and solidarity, filling in as living study halls for schooling and motivation across ages. Besides, these marvels catalyze reasonable turn of events and advance social grasping, cultivating harmony in an isolated world.

However, they likewise help us to remember the difficulties we face — environmental change, urbanization, contamination, and that's only the tip of the iceberg — that compromise their reality. In this unique situation, the marvels become a source of inspiration, encouraging us to secure and protect our legacy for people in the future.

Fundamentally, the Seven Marvels of Protection are not relics of the past but rather living responsibilities to a supportable and comprehensive future. They motivate us to embrace our obligation as stewards of culture and nature, to act with earnestness and assurance, and to pass on an enduring heritage for a long time into the future.

CHAPTER 1

The Birth of World Heritage

The Introduction of World Legacy

The idea of saving social and regular legacy locales on a worldwide scale, as far as we might be concerned today through UNESCO's Reality Legacy program, was conceived out of a squeezing need to secure and shield humankind's most cherished treasures. The narrative of the introduction of World Legacy is a story of global collaboration, a reaction to the rising dangers presented by industrialization, urbanization, and fast improvement that were jeopardizing our reality's indispensable legacy. This account follows the authentic foundation paving the way to the production of UNESCO's Reality Legacy program, its key achievements, and the early difficulties and victories that prepared for the security and protection of our planet's remarkable social and regular destinations.

Authentic Setting

To comprehend the introduction of the World Legacy program, it is fundamental to consider the authentic setting wherein it arose. The mid-twentieth century was set apart by huge international moves, the finish of frontier realms, and the post-war remaking of Europe and Asia. These progressions were joined by fast monetary development, urbanization, and the change of customary social orders. While these improvements carried success to many, they likewise had significant ramifications for social and normal legacy.

The impacts of industrialization, never-ending suburbia, and unregulated improvement were negatively affecting memorable destinations and normal scenes. Old urban communities were being annihilated to clear a path for present day foundation, unblemished conditions were being contaminated, and customary social practices were being disintegrated. In this unique circumstance, the requirement for global collaboration to secure and save the world's legacy turned out to be progressively obvious.

The Beginning of the Thought

Saving social and regular legacy on a worldwide scale can be followed back to the nineteenth 100 years. European countries, specifically, were wrestling with the difficulties presented by the quick industrialization and urbanization of the time. The Heartfelt development, which arose in light of the modern unrest, underscored the enthusiasm for nature and a nostalgic yearning for less complex, more customary times.

One of the earliest articulations of this feeling was the safeguarding of normal scenes. In 1872, the US laid out Yellowstone Public Park, the world's most memorable public park, as a safe-haven for the protection of its extraordinary geothermal highlights and normal excellence. This undeniable the start of a worldwide development to safeguard normal legacy.

The conservation of social legacy, in any case, lingered behind. It was only after the mid twentieth century that the global local area started to perceive the significance of safeguarding notable and compositional milestones. The 1912 Deal of The Hague, for instance, planned to safeguard social property during seasons of equipped struggle.

UNESCO's Job

The establishment for the World Legacy program was laid with the foundation of UNESCO itself. UNESCO, the Unified Countries Instructive, Logical and Social Association, was made in 1945 as a reaction to the pulverization of The Second Great War. Its main goal was to advance global participation in the fields of schooling, science, and culture, fully intent on building harmony through common getting it and information sharing.

UNESCO's Constitution, took on November 16, 1945, proclaimed that "the safeguarding and security of the world's social and regular legacy involves widespread concern." This acknowledgment of the significance of legacy protection set up for the production of the World Legacy program.

The Introduction of the World Legacy Program

Making a program devoted to the security of social and normal legacy picked up speed inside UNESCO during the mid 1960s. The impetus for this development was the development of the Aswan High Dam in Egypt, which compromised the old sanctuaries of Abu Simbel. Global endeavors, including an UNESCO-drove crusade, effectively moved the sanctuaries to higher ground, saving them from immersion.

The effective salvage of Abu Simbel featured the requirement for a more extensive and efficient way to deal with legacy safeguarding. It became clear that a program was expected to recognize, assign, and safeguard locales of excellent worth to humankind, both social and normal, on a worldwide scale. Subsequently, the World Legacy program started to come to fruition.

The World Legacy Show

The defining moment came on November 16, 1972, when the Overall Meeting of UNESCO embraced the World Legacy Show during its seventeenth meeting in Paris. The Show was authoritatively known as the "Show concerning the Insurance of the World Social and Regular Legacy." It laid the preparation for the precise distinguishing proof and protection of social and normal legacy destinations of all inclusive worth.

The Show presented a few pivotal ideas:

Remarkable Widespread Worth (OUV): This was the measure that a site needed to meet to be remembered for the World Legacy Rundown. It implied that a site shouldn't just be of importance to the country in which it was found yet additionally hold importance for all of mankind.

Global Collaboration: The Show underscored worldwide participation in the ID and assurance of legacy destinations. It called for cooperation among countries, specialists, and associations to accomplish its objectives.

Security of Destinations: The Show required the insurance and protection of assigned World Legacy Locales. It urged nations to lay out viable components for the protecting of their social and normal fortunes.

The reception of the World Legacy Show denoted a huge achievement throughout the entire existence of legacy safeguarding. It addressed a worldwide obligation to protecting our common social and normal legacy and perceived that the safeguarding of these fortunes rose above public limits and political contrasts.

The Debut World Legacy Rundown

The primary rundown of World Legacy Destinations was distributed in 1978, highlighting a blend of social and regular miracles. It included notorious destinations like the Galápagos Islands, Machu Picchu, Yellowstone Public Park, and the Stone Cut Houses of worship of Lalibela in Ethiopia. These locales addressed a cross-part of the world's outstanding legacy.

The consideration of normal destinations close by social ones was an outstanding element of the World Legacy program, mirroring the comprehension that the protection of regular legacy was similarly pretty much as imperative as the conservation of social legacy. This all encompassing methodology put the program aside and highlighted the interconnectedness of human culture and the climate.

Early Difficulties and Victories

In its initial years, the World Legacy program confronted different difficulties. A few nations were at first reluctant to designate their destinations because of worries about power and expected limitations ashore use. Also, the World Legacy Advisory group needed to explore the sensitive harmony between the independence of part states and the requirement for global oversight.

In spite of these difficulties, the program accomplished early triumphs. The consideration of locales like Yellowstone Public Park and Machu Picchu on the World Legacy Rundown drew worldwide consideration and brought issues to light about the significance of legacy conservation. It likewise motivated different nations to name their own remarkable destinations.

Growing the Rundown and Difficulties Ahead

Throughout the long term that followed, the World Legacy Rundown kept on growing, including a different exhibit of social and normal destinations from around the world. These locales addressed the rich embroidered artwork of mankind's set of experiences, from antiquated urban communities and archeological miracles to flawless wild regions and exceptional biological systems.

In any case, the program likewise experienced new difficulties. The effects of environmental change, unrestrained the travel industry, outfitted struggle, and political insecurity kept on compromising legacy locales. Adjusting the necessities of preservation with the interests of nearby networks and legislatures stayed an intricate undertaking.

1.1 Historical background leading to the creation of UNESCO.

Authentic Foundation Prompting the Making of UNESCO

The foundation of the Unified Countries Instructive, Logical and Social Association, otherwise called UNESCO, was a turning point throughout the entire existence of global collaboration and a reaction to the demolition of The Second Great War. To comprehend the verifiable foundation prompting the making of UNESCO, we should dig into the violent period that went before its development and investigate the vital occasions and thoughts that made ready for the introduction of this significant worldwide association.

The Result of The Second Great War and the Class of Countries

The underlying foundations of UNESCO can be followed back to the repercussions of The Second Great War and the development of the Class of Countries. The Second Great War, which seethed from 1914 to 1918, was an overwhelming struggle that left millions dead, urban communities in remains, and whole social orders damaged. Afterward, there was an aggregate craving to keep such a disastrous occasion from reoccurring.

The Class of Countries, laid out in 1920 as a forerunner to the Unified Countries, expected to advance worldwide collaboration and forestall future struggles. It perceived the significance of resolving issues connected with instruction, science, and culture for the purpose of cultivating understanding and harmony among countries. The Association's endeavors here set up for the more extensive drives that would accompany the foundation of UNESCO.

The Second Great War and the Obliteration of Social Legacy

The episode of The Second Great War in 1939 further highlighted the requirement for global participation in the domains of schooling, science, and culture. The conflict saw far and wide obliteration, including the purposeful focusing of social legacy destinations. Milestones, memorable urban communities, and social relics were decreased to rubble.

One of the most scandalous instances of social obliteration during this period was the bombarding of the noteworthy city of Guernica in Spain during the Spanish Nationwide conflict. The conscious focusing of this social place stunned the world and featured the weakness of social legacy in the midst of contention.

The Spearheading Work of the U.S. Office of Schooling

Amidst The Second Great War, a momentous drive in the US laid the foundation for UNESCO's future endeavors in training. The U.S. Office of Schooling, under the authority of John Franklin Bobbitt, sent off the "Board on Wartime Projects in Training" in 1942. This panel perceived the significance of schooling as an instrument for post-war remaking and worldwide comprehension.

The council's work prompted the distribution of the persuasive "Bobbitt Report" in 1945, which framed a dream for worldwide participation in training. It proposed the making of a "Joined Countries Instructive and Social Association" to advance harmony, security, and human nobility through training, science, and culture.

The Introduction of the Unified Countries

In 1945, as The Second Great War attracted to a nearby, world pioneers accumulated in San Francisco to draft the Contract of the Unified Countries. The Unified Countries was imagined as a replacement to the Class of Countries, with a more extensive command to advance worldwide harmony and security.

Inside the Unified Countries Sanction, there was an unmistakable acknowledgment of the significance of schooling, science, and culture in propelling the association's objectives. Article 55 of the Sanction expressed that the Assembled Countries would advance "better expectations of living, full work, and states of financial and social advancement and improvement." Article 57 explicitly referenced participation in "instructive, social, and medical issues."

The Arrangement of UNESCO

UNESCO arose as a substantial acknowledgment of the vision framed in the "Bobbitt Report" and the standards of the Unified Countries Contract. Making an association committed to schooling, science, and culture acquired boundless help during the Unified Countries Gathering on Global Association in San Francisco in 1945.

On November 16, 1945, the Constitution of UNESCO was embraced, officially laying out the association. Its main goal was explained in the preface of the Constitution:

"Since wars start in the personalities of men, it is in the personalities of men that the safeguards of harmony should be built."

This significant assertion highlighted UNESCO's obligation to building harmony through schooling, science, and culture by cultivating common figuring out, exchange, and collaboration among countries.

Key Goals and Capabilities

The Constitution of UNESCO illustrated a few critical targets and works for the association, including:

Advancing Instruction: UNESCO was entrusted with advancing instructive collaboration and admittance to schooling for all, with a specific spotlight on decreasing ignorance and propelling the ideal of free training.

Propelling Science: The association meant to advance worldwide logical joint effort and the trading of information and thoughts.

Saving Society: UNESCO was endowed with the errand of safeguarding and monitoring social legacy, both substantial and elusive, and advancing social variety.

Cultivating Correspondence: It looked to work with the free progression of thoughts and information through global correspondence and data trade.

Battling Bias and Advancing Common liberties: UNESCO was focused on combatting bias, separation, and prejudice, and to advancing admiration for basic freedoms and key opportunities.

Early Accomplishments and Difficulties

In its initial years, UNESCO left on a large number of drives to satisfy its main goal. It upheld endeavors to remake school systems in post-war Europe, worked with logical collaboration, and started social protection projects. One of its most striking early triumphs was the salvage and rebuilding of the Nubian landmarks in Egypt, which were compromised by the development of the Aswan High Dam.

Be that as it may, UNESCO additionally confronted early difficulties, including political strains during the Virus War. The withdrawal of the US and the Unified Realm from the association in 1984 and 1985, separately, because of seen issues of blunder and politicization, represented a huge misfortune.

Extending Its Command

Throughout the long term, UNESCO's command extended to address arising worldwide difficulties. It widened its work to incorporate media improvement, the advancement of orientation equity, ecological manageability, and the defending of elusive social legacy.

The association assumed a significant part in the foundation of the World Legacy program, as well as drives prefer the Man and the Biosphere program.

In 1993, UNESCO sent off the World Meeting on Advanced education, which prompted the reception of the World Statement on Advanced education for the 21st Hundred years. This statement underscored the significance of advanced education in a quickly impacting world and the requirement for long lasting learning.

UNESCO in the 21st Hundred years

UNESCO keeps on assuming a vital part in addressing worldwide difficulties connected with schooling, science, culture, correspondence, and data. Its work stretches out to regions, for example, environmental change schooling, media education, and the security of social variety in the computerized age.

The association stays resolved to its establishing standards of harmony, global participation, and the advancement of common freedoms. It fills in as a gathering for discourse and coordinated effort among part states and assumes an essential part in propelling the Feasible Improvement Objectives (SDGs) of the Unified Countries.

1.2 The origins of the World Heritage Convention.

The Starting points of the World Legacy Show

The World Legacy Show, formally known as the "Show concerning the Security of the World Social and Regular Legacy," remains as a demonstration of mankind's obligation to defending its most remarkable social and normal fortunes. The starting points of this global deal can be followed back to a developing consciousness of the need to secure and safeguard the world's legacy for people in the future. This story investigates the authentic setting and occasions prompting the formation of the World Legacy Show and its resulting influence on the protection of our worldwide legacy.

A World Scarred by War and Change

The mid-twentieth century was a time of significant worldwide change and disturbance. Arising out of the demolition of The Second Great War, the world saw the destroying of pilgrim domains, the remaking of war-torn Europe and Asia, and the fast development of industrialization and urbanization. This time of change brought both exceptional success and new difficulties to the front.

One of the difficulties that arose during this time was the fast debasement and obliteration of social and normal legacy destinations. Memorable urban areas were leveled to clear a path for present day improvement, unblemished scenes confronted natural debasement, and conventional societies were in danger of being disintegrated notwithstanding fast change.

Thus, the requirement for global collaboration to safeguard and save the world's legacy turned out to be progressively obvious.

Early Endeavors to Shield Legacy

Preceding the formation of the World Legacy Show, there were a few global endeavors to safeguard social and normal legacy. Prominent models include:

1. **The 1912 Deal of The Hague:** This settlement expected to safeguard social property during seasons of furnished struggle and was a reaction to the broad social harm brought about by The Second Great War.
2. **The 1930 Athens Sanction for the Reclamation of Memorable Landmarks:** This contract framed standards for the rebuilding of noteworthy landmarks and laid out the requirement for global cooperation in legacy safeguarding.

3. **The 1943 Global Galleries Office (IMO) Meeting:** Held during The Second Great War, this gathering examined the insurance of social legacy during seasons of contention and the recuperation of stolen from social fortunes.

While these early endeavors laid significant preparation, they were to a great extent zeroed in on the security of legacy during equipped contentions and didn't address the more extensive difficulties presented by urbanization, industrialization, and improvement.

The Introduction of the Thought

Making a complete worldwide structure for the security of both social and normal legacy started to come to fruition during the twentieth 100 years. A few critical occasions and people assumed significant parts in supporting this thought:

1. **The Aswan High Dam Emergency (1954-1960):** One of the impetuses for the production of the World Legacy Show was the development of the Aswan High Dam in Egypt, which represented a danger to the old sanctuaries of Abu Simbel. A global mission drove by UNESCO effectively activated help and assets to migrate these sanctuaries to higher ground, protecting them for people in the future.

2. **The Vision of Sir Bernard Feilden:** English draftsman and preservation-ist Sir Bernard Feilden assumed a critical part in molding the idea of worldwide legacy security. He upheld for a worldwide deal that would include both social and normal legacy and proposed the foundation of an "Global Place for Preservation" to facilitate these endeavors.

3. **The Impact of Worldwide Specialists:** UNESCO met a progression of master gatherings and meetings during the 1960s to examine the conservation of legacy. These social affairs united specialists in the fields of culture and nature preservation and added to the definition of the World Legacy Show.

The Formation of the World Legacy Show

Making a devoted worldwide instrument for the security of social and regular legacy picked up speed inside UNESCO during the mid 1960s. This force finished in the reception of the World Legacy Show on November 16, 1972, during the seventeenth meeting of the Overall Gathering of UNESCO in Paris.

The Show presented a few noteworthy ideas that keep on forming legacy conservation right up 'til now:

1. **Extraordinary Widespread Worth (OUV):** The Show underscored that for a site to be remembered for the World Legacy Show, it should meet the basis of "exceptional general worth." This implied that a site shouldn't just be of importance to the country in which it was found yet in addition hold importance for all of humankind.
2. **Worldwide Collaboration:** The Show called for global participation in the distinguishing proof, security, and safeguarding of legacy destinations. It perceived that the obligation regarding protecting these destinations rose above public limits.
3. **Insurance of Destinations:** The Show stressed the security and protection of assigned World Legacy Locales. It encouraged nations to lay out viable components for protecting their social and normal fortunes.

The Debut World Legacy Rundown
The primary rundown of World Legacy Destinations was distributed in 1978, highlighting a different scope of social and normal miracles from around the world. It included notorious locales like the Galápagos Islands, Machu Picchu, Yellowstone Public Park, and the Stone Cut Chapels of Lalibela in Ethiopia. These locales were perceived as having "extraordinary all inclusive worth" and were viewed as a cross-part of the world's uncommon legacy.

The incorporation of normal locales close by social ones was a prominent element of the World Legacy Show, mirroring the comprehension that the protection of regular legacy was similarly pretty much as crucial as the conservation of social legacy. This comprehensive methodology highlighted the interconnectedness of human culture and the climate.

Early Difficulties and Triumphs
In its initial years, the World Legacy program confronted different difficulties. A few nations were at first reluctant to choose their locales because of worries about sway and expected limitations ashore use. Moreover, the World Legacy Board of trustees needed to explore the fragile harmony between the independence of part states and the requirement for global oversight.

Notwithstanding these difficulties, the program accomplished early victories. The incorporation of destinations like Yellowstone Public Park and Machu Picchu on the World Legacy Rundown drew worldwide consideration and brought issues to light about the significance of legacy conservation. It likewise enlivened different nations to select their own extraordinary destinations.

Growing the Rundown and Difficulties Ahead
Throughout the long term that followed, the World Legacy Rundown kept on extending, incorporating a different exhibit of social and regular locales from around the world. These destinations addressed the rich woven artwork of

mankind's set of experiences, from antiquated urban communities and archeological marvels to flawless wild regions and special environments.

Nonetheless, the program additionally experienced new difficulties. The effects of environmental change, uncontrolled the travel industry, equipped struggle, and political shakiness kept on undermining legacy locales. Adjusting the necessities of preservation with the interests of neighborhood networks and states stayed a mind boggling try.

1.3 The first World Heritage Sites and their importance.

The Principal World Legacy Locales and Their Significance

The assignment of the primary World Legacy Locales in 1978 denoted a notable second in the worldwide work to save and safeguard our planet's most extraordinary social and normal legacy. These debut destinations, painstakingly chose for their remarkable general worth, embody the rich variety of mankind's set of experiences and the unrivaled excellence and biological meaning of the regular world. In this story, we dig into the accounts and meaning of the primary World Legacy Locales and their persevering through significance to humankind.

Galápagos Islands - A Living Research center of Development

The Galápagos Islands, arranged in the Pacific Sea off the shore of Ecuador, were among the initial 12 destinations engraved on the World Legacy Rundown. These islands, known for their noteworthy biodiversity and one of a kind environments, assumed a significant part in molding Charles Darwin's hypothesis of development by normal determination.

Significance:

Logical Importance: The Galápagos Islands offer a living research facility for the investigation of development. The assorted cluster of species, large numbers of which are found no place else on The planet, furnished Darwin with urgent experiences into the cycles of variation and regular determination.

Preservation: The assignment of the Galápagos Islands as a World Legacy Site carried worldwide regard for their protection needs. Endeavors to safeguard this delicate biological system have since been increased, assisting with protecting this regular miracle for people in the future.

Instruction and Exploration: The Galápagos Islands keep on being a center point for logical examination and schooling, drawing in scientists and understudies from around the world. These investigations add to how we might interpret biology, biodiversity, and the effects of environmental change.

Machu Picchu - The Lost City of the Inca

Machu Picchu, settled high in the Andes Piles of Peru, is an archeological wonder that offers a window into the old Inca civilization. This very much protected city, concealed in the mists, is a demonstration of the design and designing ability of its manufacturers.

Significance:

Social Legacy: Machu Picchu addresses a zenith of Inca engineering and culture. Its complicated stone designs, terraced rural fields, and stately locales give experiences into the everyday existence and profound acts of the Inca public.

The travel industry and Economy: The assignment as a World Legacy Site has made Machu Picchu perhaps of the most notorious and visited archeological site on the planet. It has turned into a critical driver of the travel industry and monetary improvement in the district.

Conservation: The worldwide acknowledgment of Machu Picchu's significance has prompted expanded endeavors to secure and save the site. This incorporates measures to alleviate the effect of the travel industry, for example, guest quantities and preservation projects.

Yellowstone Public Park - A Characteristic Wonderland

Yellowstone Public Park, found essentially in the U.S. provinces of Wyoming, Montana, and Idaho, is a characteristic wonderland overflowing with geothermal highlights, unblemished scenes, and bountiful untamed life. It was the world's most memorable public park and became one of the principal World Legacy Locales.

Significance:

Geographical Wonders: Yellowstone is home to additional fountains, underground aquifers, and warm elements than elsewhere on The planet. These special land ponders offer important experiences into the World's cycles.

Biodiversity: The recreation area is a safe-haven for a different scope of animal types, including famous megafauna like wild bears, wolves, and buffalo. Its biological systems are fundamental for preservation endeavors in the district.

Entertainment and Instruction: Yellowstone fills in as a center point for open air diversion, logical examination, and natural schooling. It offers valuable open doors for guests to interface with nature and find out about protection.

Rock-Slashed Houses of worship of Lalibela - Ethiopia's Otherworldly Legacy

The Stone Slashed Houses of worship of Lalibela, situated in Ethiopia, are an exceptional compositional accomplishment cut straightforwardly into the strong stone. These 11 middle age temples, with their mind boggling carvings and strict importance, are a demonstration of human innovativeness and dedication.

Significance:

Otherworldly and Social Importance: Lalibela is a focal point of Ethiopian Conventional Christianity, and its temples are viewed as holy journey destinations. They hold profound strict and social significance for Ethiopians and the worldwide Christian people group.

Structural Wonder: The stone cut places of worship of Lalibela are a demonstration of the creativity of their manufacturers. The accuracy and creativity showed in their development keep on moving stunningness.

Conservation and Reclamation: Acknowledgment as a World Legacy Site has worked with endeavors to save and reestablish these old holy places. Protection drives guarantee that people in the future can see the value in this exceptional building legacy.

The Significance of the Principal World Legacy Locales

The primary World Legacy Locales hold an extraordinary spot in the shared mindset of humankind. They represent the obligation to secure and save our common social and normal fortunes. Past their inborn worth, these locales have had a sweeping effect:

Worldwide Mindfulness: The assignment of the primary World Legacy Locales carried worldwide thoughtfulness regarding the significance of legacy protection. It highlighted the interconnectedness of human culture and the climate.

Motivation and Learning: These locales keep on moving amazement and miracle, filling in as instructive assets for individuals, everything being equal. They are spots where guests can find out about history, culture, biology, and the requirement for mindful stewardship.

Practical The travel industry: A large number of these locales have become significant vacationer locations, adding to neighborhood economies while likewise introducing difficulties connected with overseeing guest influence. They represent the fragile harmony among the travel industry and protection.

Preservation and Insurance: The main World Legacy Destinations have been at the front of protection endeavors. Their acknowledgment as around the world huge spots has prompted expanded assets and global collaboration to shield their trustworthiness.

Social Trade: World Legacy Locales act as extensions among societies and countries. They cultivate exchange and participation among different networks, advancing comprehension and regard.

CHAPTER 2

Cultural Heritage Wonders

Social Legacy Miracles: Protecting Our Common Inheritance

Social legacy ponders are a demonstration of the wealth and variety of human development. These wonderful locales, ancient rarities, and customs take the stand concerning the inventiveness, innovativeness, and social articulations of social orders across overall setting. They give a window into the past and act as a wellspring of motivation, character, and understanding for present and people in the future. In this investigation of social legacy ponders, we will travel through a portion of the world's most notorious destinations and dive into the meaning of protecting these fortunes.

The Force of Social Legacy

Social legacy envelops an expansive range of unmistakable and immaterial articulations of human innovativeness and custom. It incorporates archeological destinations, memorable structures, works of art, original copies, dialects, music, legends, customs, and that's just the beginning. The force of social legacy lies in its capacity to:

Interface Us to Our Foundations: Social legacy assists people and networks with associating with their set of experiences, parentage, and social roots. It cultivates a feeling of having a place and personality.

Advance Getting it: Social legacy spans holes between various social orders and encourages diverse comprehension. It is a wellspring of sympathy, permitting us to see the value in the encounters and viewpoints of others.

Move Imagination: Social legacy fills in as a wellspring of motivation for craftsmen, scholars, and makers. It energizes advancement by attracting from the past to illuminate the present and shape what's to come.

Save Customs: It shields conventional practices, dialects, and customs, guaranteeing they are gone down through ages. This conservation keeps up with social variety.

Support Practical The travel industry: Numerous social legacy destinations draw in guests from around the world, adding to neighborhood economies. Practical the travel industry can produce income for protection endeavors.

Notable Social Legacy Marvels

1. **The Incomparable Mass of China**

   The Incomparable Mass of China is one of the world's most notable social legacy ponders. This gigantic stronghold extends north of 13,000 miles and was worked over hundreds of years to shield China from intrusions. Its verifiable and structural importance, alongside its sheer scale, makes it an image of Chinese development and flexibility.

   Significance:

   Verifiable Importance: The Incomparable Wall exemplifies China's long history of dynastic rule and struggle with adjoining states.

   Structural Wonder: Its development procedures and designing accomplishments keep on awing scientists and travelers the same.

   Vacation spot: It draws a great many guests every year, supporting the travel industry related businesses and nearby economies.

2. **Machu Picchu, Peru**

   Machu Picchu, frequently alluded to as the "Lost City of the Inca," is a stunning archeological site situated in the Andes Piles of Peru. This old city was implicit the fifteenth 100 years and is eminent for its modern dry-stone development and its dazzling area high in the mountains.

   Significance:

   Building Wonder: Machu Picchu exhibits the designing and compositional ability of the Inca human progress.

   Social Importance: It gives knowledge into the everyday existence and profound acts of the Inca public.

   The travel industry and Economy: The site has turned into a significant vacation spot, helping the nearby economy and supporting protection endeavors.

3. **The Memorable Focal point of Rome, Italy**

   Rome, frequently alluded to as the "Everlasting City," is a living demonstration of the magnificence of the Roman Realm and the development of Western civilization. Its notable community, including notorious tourist spots like the Colosseum, the Roman Discussion, and the Pantheon, is an UNESCO World Legacy Site.

   Significance:

   Social Progression: Rome's noteworthy focus jam layers of history, from antiquated Rome to the Renaissance and then some.

   Building Fortunes: It houses a portion of the world's most famous compositional wonders.

The travel industry Center: A great many sightseers visit Rome yearly to investigate its social legacy, adding to the city's economy.

4. **The Pyramids of Egypt**

The Pyramids of Egypt, including the Incomparable Pyramid of Giza, are persevering through images of old Egyptian development. These epic designs, worked as burial chambers for pharaohs, are a demonstration of the designing, cosmology, and numerical information on the time.

Significance:

Structural Wonders: The accuracy and size of the pyramids keep on surprising specialists and guests.

Social Importance: They are an impression of the strict convictions and practices of old Egyptians.

The travel industry and Personality: The pyramids are a significant vacation spot and an image of Egyptian character.

5. **Angkor Wat, Cambodia**

Angkor Wat is a shocking sanctuary complex in Cambodia that filled in as the capital of the Khmer Domain in the twelfth 100 years. It is famous for its perplexing design, many-sided bas-reliefs, and the glory of its focal sanctuary.

Significance:

Structural Show-stopper: Angkor Wat is a work of art of Khmer engineering and an image of Cambodia.

Social and Strict Importance: It mirrors the combination of Hindu and Buddhist strict customs in the locale.

The travel industry and Protection: It draws in vacationers from around the world, adding to the nearby economy and supporting rebuilding endeavors.

The Difficulties of Conservation

While social legacy ponders are a wellspring of motivation and pride, they likewise face various difficulties:

Regular Rot: The progression of time, climate, and cataclysmic events can prompt the disintegration of social legacy locales and curios.

Human Effect: Congestion, contamination, and deficient foundation at famous destinations can harm the very loves travelers come to see.

Struggle and Defacement: Outfitted struggle and destructive incidents can prompt the annihilation of social legacy, as found on account of Palmyra in Syria.

Unlawful Dealing: The unlawful exchange of social curios can prompt the deficiency of important legacy things.

Environmental Change: Rising ocean levels and outrageous climate occasions undermine seaside legacy destinations and biological systems.

The Job of Safeguarding and Preservation

Protection and preservation endeavors are critical in shielding social legacy ponders for people in the future. These endeavors include:

Reclamation: Talented rebuilding work can turn around harm and rot, returning social fortunes to their previous greatness.

Protection Arranging: Cautious preparation and the board are vital for offset the travel industry with conservation needs.

Schooling and Mindfulness: Raising public mindfulness about the significance of social legacy protection can prompt capable the travel industry and backing for preservation.

Global Participation: Cooperative endeavors including countries, associations, and specialists can shield legacy locales from dangers like illegal dealing and furnished struggle.

Environment Versatility: Carrying out methodologies to moderate the effects of environmental change on legacy locales, particularly those in beach front regions, is fundamental.

2.1 Exploration of iconic cultural heritage sites:

Investigation of Notorious Social Legacy Locales: An Excursion Through Time

Investigating notorious social legacy locales resembles setting out on an excursion through time, venturing into the strides of our precursors, and drenching ourselves in the marvels of human development. These locales are verifiable relics as well as living demonstrations of the imaginativeness, inventiveness, and social extravagance of social orders across the ages. In this investigation, we will navigate a portion of the world's most celebrated social legacy destinations, uncovering their accounts and the significant importance they hold.

The Colosseum, Rome, Italy

The Colosseum, otherwise called the Flavian Amphitheater, remains as a great image of old Rome's designing ability and the glory of its diversion culture. Underlying the first century Promotion, this curved amphitheater could hold up to 80,000 onlookers and facilitated gladiatorial challenges, creature chases, and dramatic exhibitions.

Importance:

Design Wonder: The Colosseum's inventive development procedures, including the utilization of curves and cement, were pivotal for now is the right time and have affected engineering for a really long time.

Social Importance: It mirrors the centrality of public displays in Roman culture and the longing to grandstand supreme power.

Vacation spot: The Colosseum draws a huge number of guests yearly, giving a brief look into old Roman life and culture.

The Taj Mahal, Agra, India

The Taj Mahal, frequently alluded to as the "Crown of Castles," is a wonderful white marble sepulcher that stands as a demonstration of persevering through affection. Underlying the seventeenth hundred years by Ruler Shah Jahan in memory of his darling spouse Mumtaz Mahal, it is a work of art of Mughal engineering.

Importance:

Building Magnificence: The Taj Mahal's even plan, complex marble decorate work, and rich nurseries make a stunning and amicable organization.

Image of Adoration: It exemplifies the timeless love between Shah Jahan and Mumtaz Mahal, making it a widespread image of commitment.

Social Legacy: The Taj Mahal is an UNESCO World Legacy Site and a persevering through social fortune of India.

The Acropolis of Athens, Greece

The Acropolis of Athens, roosted on a rough slope, is an image of old Greek human progress and the origination of a majority rules system. It incorporates notable designs, for example, the Parthenon, a sanctuary devoted to the goddess Athena, and the Erechtheion, known for its Caryatid sections.

Importance:

Compositional Victory: The Parthenon epitomizes old style Greek design, including Doric segments and complex friezes that describe legends and history.

Social and Verifiable Importance: The Acropolis addresses the apex of Greek social and political accomplishments and the introduction of Western civilization.

Vacation destination: It draws in guests from around the world who come to respect its verifiable and structural magnificence.

The Incomparable Mass of China

The Incomparable Mass of China is a gigantic stronghold that traverses great many miles across northern China. It was worked over hundreds of years to safeguard against attacks by migrant clans. This momentous construction is certainly not a solitary wall yet a progression of walls and fortresses.

Importance:

Designing Wonder: The Incomparable Wall's development included an astounding measure of work and assets, displaying the designing ability of old China.

Verifiable Importance: It mirrors China's long history of dynastic rule and its procedures for protecting against outside dangers.

Worldwide Symbol: The Incomparable Wall is perceived overall as a famous image of China and quite possibly of mankind's most noteworthy design accomplishment.

Petra, Jordan

Petra, frequently called the "Rose City," is a verifiable and archeological miracle concealed in the deserts of Jordan. Cut into the rose-red bluffs of southern Jordan, it was the capital of the Nabatean Realm in the fourth century BC.

Importance:

Compositional Wonder: Petra's stone cut design, including the renowned Depository and Religious community, exhibits the designing abilities of the Nabateans.

Social Legacy: It addresses the gathering point of different societies, as confirmed by its Greco-Roman, Egyptian, and Middle Eastern impacts.

Lost City: Petra was lost toward the Western world for a really long time until its rediscovery in the nineteenth hundred years, adding to its persona and charm.

The Incomparable Pyramids of Giza, Egypt

The Incomparable Pyramids of Giza, worked a long time back, are persevering through images of old Egypt's compositional and designing accomplishments. These fantastic designs filled in as burial chambers for pharaohs and are joined by the perplexing Sphinx.

Importance:

Building Win: The exact development of the pyramids, lining up with the cardinal marks of the compass, stays a subject of interest and study.

Social and Verifiable Importance: They are a demonstration of Egypt's perplexing strict convictions, high level science, and worship for its rulers.

Vacation spot: The Incomparable Pyramids draw in large number of guests every year, making them a foundation of Egypt's travel industry.

The Alhambra, Granada, Spain

The Alhambra, a castle and stronghold complex, is a gem of Islamic design and an image of Spain's multicultural history. It was worked during the Nasrid Tradition in the thirteenth and fourteenth hundreds of years.

Importance:

Structural Magnificence: The Alhambra is prestigious for its many-sided plaster work, beautiful tiles, and quiet gardens.

Social Combination: It mirrors the conjunction of Islamic, Christian, and Jewish societies in middle age Spain, known as Al-Andalus.

World Legacy Site: The Alhambra is perceived as an UNESCO World Legacy Site, safeguarding its verifiable and social significance.

Meaning of Investigating Social Legacy Destinations

Investigating famous social legacy destinations is an excursion that rises above general setting. It permits us to:

Interface with History: Visiting these destinations gives a substantial association with the past, empowering us to see the value in the accomplishments and difficulties of our precursors.

Social Enhancement: Drenching ourselves in different societies and design wonders expands our viewpoints and extends our social comprehension.

Protection: The travel industry produces income that can be reinvested in the conservation and upkeep of these locales for people in the future.

Motivation: These destinations move workmanship, writing, and development by filling in as a wellspring of imagination and thoughts.

Cultivating Worldwide Comprehension: Social legacy destinations advance culturally diverse discourse and grasping, encouraging a feeling of shared mankind.

2.2 The Pyramids of Giza, Egypt

The Pyramids of Giza, Egypt: An Immortal Wonder

The Pyramids of Giza are maybe the most famous and persevering through images of antiquated Egypt's structural and designing ability. Arranged on the Giza Level, right external advanced Cairo, these amazing designs have enamored the world's creative mind for centuries. They stand as demonstrations of the glory of a progress that prospered a long time back and proceed to perplex and move guests from around the globe.

The Grand Set of three

The Giza Level is home to three essential pyramids, each developed for an alternate pharaoh of Egypt's Old Realm:

1. **The Incomparable Pyramid of Khufu (Cheops)**

   The Incomparable Pyramid, initially remaining at 146.6 meters (481 feet), was the tallest man-made structure on the planet for more than 3,800 years. Worked for Pharaoh Khufu (otherwise called Cheops), it is the biggest and generally famous of the Giza pyramids.

   The accuracy with which it was developed, adjusted to the cardinal places of the compass, keeps on amazing designers and antiquarians.

   Importance:

   Building Wonder: The Incomparable Pyramid's development methods stay a subject of interest and discussion, with speculations going from the utilization of slopes to cutting edge math.

   Social and Verifiable Importance: It filled in as a burial place for Pharaoh Khufu and was a focal point of old Egyptian strict convictions encompassing existence in the wake of death.

   Worldwide Fascination: The Incomparable Pyramid is a significant vacationer location, drawing in great many guests every year who wonder about its overwhelming presence and verifiable importance.

2. **The Pyramid of Khafre (Chephren)**

   The Pyramid of Khafre, somewhat more limited than the Incomparable Pyramid, is many times perceived by the packaging stones that still to some extent decorate its pinnacle. It was worked for Pharaoh Khafre, trusted by some to be Khufu's replacement and stepbrother.

Importance:

Notorious Sphinx: Neighboring the Pyramid of Khafre stands the cryptic Incredible Sphinx, a titanic limestone sculpture with the body of a lion and the top of a pharaoh, possible addressing Khafre.

Arrangement and Evenness: The Pyramid of Khafre, alongside its encompassing designs, features the accuracy and balance normal for Egyptian pyramid buildings.

3. **The Pyramid of Menkaure**

The littlest of the three pyramids on the Giza Level, the Pyramid of Menkaure, was developed for Pharaoh Menkaure. It remains at 65 meters (213 feet) tall and is prominent for the utilization of stone in its development.

Importance:

Engineering Subtlety: The Pyramid of Menkaure highlights the utilization of rock and wonderful sets of three of sculptures in its sanctuary buildings.

Authentic Viewpoint: It gives bits of knowledge into the development of pyramid plan and development during the Old Realm.

Structural Wonders

The development of the Pyramids of Giza stays a subject of interest and wonder. These goliath structures were constructed utilizing a mix of resourcefulness, science, and a colossal workforce. A few vital structural elements and secrets include:

Exact Arrangement: The pyramids are strikingly lined up with the cardinal marks of the compass, a demonstration of the Egyptians' high level galactic information.

Designing Accomplishments: The development of the pyramids included the exact arrangement of monstrous stone blocks, some gauging a few tons, utilizing simple instruments. Hypotheses about the development techniques keep on being discussed, with some proposing the utilization of straight or crisscrossing slopes.

Inward Chambers: Each pyramid contains inward chambers and ways, a considerable lot of which are lined up with heavenly occasions, conceivably mirroring the Egyptian faith in the pharaoh's excursion to eternity.

Packaging Stones: The external packaging stones, initially made of profoundly cleaned Tura limestone, reflected daylight and made a stunning impact. The greater part of these packaging stones have been taken out over the long run, however a couple can in any case be seen on the Pyramid of Khafre.

Imagery and Convictions

The Pyramids of Giza were not simply design accomplishments; they held significant social and strict importance in old Egypt:

Burial chamber of Pharaohs: The main role of the pyramids was to act as great burial chambers for pharaohs. These gigantic designs were accepted to work with the pharaoh's excursion to the great beyond.

Arrangement with Powers of providence: The format and arrangement of the pyramids might have been connected to divine bodies and the pharaoh's relationship with divinities and the universe.

Strict Ceremonies: The pyramid buildings included sanctuaries, thorough-fares, and more modest pyramids for the pharaoh's relatives. These designs assumed a focal part in strict functions and contributions to respect the departed pharaoh.

Protection and Safeguarding

The Pyramids of Giza have confronted various difficulties throughout the long term, including regular rot, defacement, and changes in environment. To save these ageless wonders, protection endeavors are continuous:

Rebuilding: Talented reclamation work expects to fix harm brought about by time, enduring, and contamination while safeguarding the uprightness of the first designs.

Traveler The board: Supportable the travel industry rehearses, for example, restricting guest numbers and executing guest rules, assist with alleviating the effect of pedestrian activity.

Worldwide Importance: Perceived as an UNESCO World Legacy Site starting around 1979, the Pyramids of Giza are praised as a common legacy of mankind, with global endeavors to guarantee their security.

2.3 The Great Wall of China.

The Incomparable Mass of China: A Landmark to Old Designing and Safeguard

The Incomparable Mass of China, perhaps of the most notable and great structural miracle on the planet, remains as a demonstration of human inventiveness, assurance, and the persevering through soul of a country. This huge stronghold, frequently alluded to as the "longest graveyard on The planet," has entranced students of history, voyagers, and pioneers for quite a long time. Traversing large number of miles and hundreds of years of history, the Incomparable Mass of China is something other than a wall; it is an image of China's rich social legacy and an exceptional accomplishment of designing and protection.

A Great Construction

1. **Monstrous Length and Scale**
   The Incomparable Mass of China extends more than 13,000 miles (21,196 kilometers), making it perhaps of the most broad design try ever. It navigates different landscape, including deserts, mountains, and meadows, across northern China.

2. Verifiable Layers

The development of the Incomparable Wall spread over different administrations and hundreds of years, with beginnings tracing all the way back to the seventh century BC. It went through various developments, redesigns, and fortresses under different Chinese heads and traditions, including the Qin, Han, and Ming Administrations.

Engineering Wonders

The Incomparable Mass of China is definitely not a solitary, uniform construction but instead an assortment of walls, lookouts, and fortresses. Its structural elements are a demonstration of the development and designing ability of old China:

1. **Materials and Development**
   The wall was built utilizing different materials, including earth, wood, blocks, and stone. Its development strategies advanced over the long haul, integrating progressed designing ideas like braces, curves, and escarpments.
2. **Lookouts and Sign Flames**
   Great many lookouts were decisively positioned along the wall to give post focuses and to house posts. Signal flames were utilized to communicate alerts and messages across immense distances.
3. **Vital Passes and Doors**

The wall was braced with decisively situated passes and doors that considered controlled admittance and filled in as protective chokepoints.

The Reason and Importance

The Incomparable Mass of China filled different needs over now is the ideal time, and its importance goes a long ways past safeguard:

1. **Protection Against Attacks**
   The basic role of the wall was to protect against intrusions by migrant clans, especially the Xiongnu, Mongols, and Manchus. It gave an impressive obstruction and offered early admonition of looming assaults.
2. **Image of Public Solidarity**
   The Incomparable Mass of China represented the solidarity of the Chinese public and their assurance to safeguard their country. It turned into a wellspring of public pride and character.
3. **Social and Authentic Fortune**

Assigned as an UNESCO World Legacy Site, the Incomparable Mass of China is commended as an indispensable piece of China's social legacy. It encapsulates the authentic and engineering accomplishments of the Chinese public.

Difficulties and Safeguarding

The Incomparable Mass of China, in spite of its hearty development, has confronted various difficulties throughout the long term, including regular rot, defacing, and infringement:

1. **Regular Rot**
   Enduring, disintegration, and vegetation development have negatively affected areas of the wall. Reclamation endeavors are progressing to save its trustworthiness.
2. **Traveler Effect**
   The notoriety of the Incomparable Wall as a traveler objective has brought about expanded people walking through and wear on specific segments. Feasible the travel industry rehearses, for example, guest restricts and controlled admittance, are being carried out.
3. **Natural Dangers**

Certain portions of the wall face natural dangers, remembering dust storms for desert districts and avalanches in bumpy regions. Environmental change and air contamination likewise present long haul difficulties.

Heritage and Worldwide Acknowledgment

The Incomparable Mass of China's getting through inheritance stretches out past its verifiable and engineering importance:

1. **Image of China**
   It is an image of China's rich history and social legacy, encapsulating the strength and solidarity of its kin.
2. **Worldwide Symbol**
   Perceived as one of the New Seven Marvels of the World, the Incomparable Mass of China draws in large number of guests from around the world, adding to China's travel industry.
3. **Social Trade**

The Incomparable Wall fills in as an extension for social trade and discourse among China and the global local area. It encourages a more profound comprehension of China's set of experiences and culture.

2.4 Machu Picchu, Peru.

Machu Picchu, Peru: The Perplexing Lost City

Settled high in the Andes Piles of Peru, Machu Picchu remains as quite possibly of the most confounding and amazing archeological site on the planet. Frequently alluded to as the "Lost City of the Inca," this old fortification is a demonstration of the structural virtuoso of the Inca civilization and keeps on charming guests with its shocking magnificence and verifiable importance.

Engineering Wonders

1. **Perplexing Dry-Stone Development**
   Machu Picchu is eminent for its complex dry-stone development, where monstrous stone blocks were masterfully cut and fitted together without the utilization of mortar. The accuracy and expertise showed in the development of its structures and porches are a demonstration of the designing ability of the Inca.
2. **Cosmic Arrangement**

A few designs inside Machu Picchu are lined up with cosmic accuracy. Strikingly, the Intihuatana stone, frequently called the "Hitching Post of the Sun," filled in as a cosmic observatory and stylized site, exhibiting the Inca's high level information on heavenly occasions.

Social Importance

1. **Profound Center**
   Machu Picchu was reasonable built during the fifteenth 100 years as a regal domain for the Inca head Pachacuti. Its area in the midst of stunning regular magnificence, encompassed by lavish terraced fields and the tough Andes, indicates its otherworldly and social importance as a retreat and stately focus.
2. **Inca Religion and Ceremonies**

The design of Machu Picchu incorporates sanctuaries, courts, and ceremonial chambers, mirroring the Inca's strict convictions and practices. The site's combination with the normal scene, including the hallowed Huayna Picchu mountain, proposes a significant association with the universe and the land.

Verifiable Secrets

Notwithstanding broad examination and investigation, Machu Picchu keeps on holding secrets and unanswered inquiries:

1. **Deserting and Rediscovery**
   Machu Picchu was deserted during the Spanish triumph, its motivation and presence blurring from authentic records. It stayed stowed away from

the Western world until its rediscovery by American history specialist and pilgrim Hiram Bingham in 1911.

2. **Reason and Capability**

While accepted to have filled in as a magnificent domain and strict site, the exact reason and capability of Machu Picchu remain subjects of academic discussion. A few speculations recommend it might play had an impact in cosmic perceptions or as a journey objective.

Safeguarding and UNESCO Acknowledgment

Machu Picchu's amazing conservation can be credited to its distant area and restricted openness to the components. In 1983, it was assigned an UNESCO World Legacy Site, perceiving its social and verifiable importance. Endeavors to safeguard the site and oversee the travel industry have since been laid out to guarantee its proceeded with uprightness.

Guest Experience

Machu Picchu invites travelers from around the world who come to respect its excellence and unwind its secrets. Guests can investigate the terraced farming fields, meander through antiquated stone designs, and wonder about the amazing vistas of the encompassing mountains and valleys.

2.5 The Acropolis of Athens, Greece.

The Acropolis of Athens, Greece: A Reference point of Old Brightness

Roosted magnificently on a rough slope sitting above the city of Athens, the Acropolis remains as a persevering through image of old Greek civilization and the support of Western culture. This archeological wonder, with its famous designs like the Parthenon and the Erechtheion, is a demonstration of the engineering virtuoso and social meaning of the Greeks. It keeps on moving wonderment and appreciation as one of the world's most notorious legacy locales.

Compositional Magnum opus

1. **The Parthenon**

   The Parthenon, committed to the goddess Athena, is the most celebrated structure on the Acropolis. Its notorious Doric sections and unpredictable friezes, embellished with models portraying Greek fantasies and legends, epitomize old style Greek engineering. The Parthenon's plan exemplifies the quest for balance and extent, making a persevering through design work of art.

2. **The Erechtheion**

The Erechtheion, one more wonderful design on the Acropolis, is known for its Caryatid segments, etched female figures filling in as engineering upholds.

This sanctuary was committed to both Athena and Poseidon and is a compositional marvel by its own doing, with its various levels and perplexing plan.

Social and Verifiable Importance

1. **Origination of A majority rules system**
   The Acropolis is in many cases thought about the origination of a vote based system, as it was a focal get-together spot for Athenians to examine political matters and go with choices that molded the administration of the city-state.
2. **Social Articulation**
   It filled in as a center for creative and scholarly pursuits, lodging sanctuaries, theaters, and safe-havens committed to different divine beings and goddesses. It was likewise the site of the eminent Dionysia celebration, commending theater and emotional expressions.
3. **Folklore and Religion**

The Acropolis was accepted to be the sacrosanct home of the city's supporter goddess, Athena. Its sanctuaries and special stepped areas were utilized for strict services and contributions, mirroring the well established strict convictions of the Greeks.

Difficulties and Conservation

The Acropolis has confronted various difficulties throughout the long term, including wars, catastrophic events, and metropolitan turn of events. Its conservation and rebuilding have been continuous for a really long time, with careful endeavors to guarantee the site's respectability.

UNESCO Acknowledgment

In 1987, the Acropolis of Athens was assigned as an UNESCO World Legacy Site, recognizing its uncommon social and verifiable importance. This acknowledgment has prompted expanded global endeavors to safeguard and protect this notable site.

Guest Experience

The Acropolis is available to guests who come from around the world to respect its structural magnificence and submerge themselves in the rich history and culture it addresses. The site offers all encompassing perspectives on Athens, causing it a stunning encounter for all who to rise its blessed grounds.

2.6 The architectural and historical significance of each site.

The Engineering and Authentic Meaning of Famous Legacy Destinations

Notorious legacy destinations like the Pyramids of Giza, the Incomparable Mass of China, Machu Picchu, and the Acropolis of Athens each hold significant design and authentic importance. These locales are exceptional in their development as well as in the accounts they tell about the civic establishments that made them.

Pyramids of Giza, Egypt

Compositional Importance:

Designing Wonder: The Pyramids of Giza are a demonstration of old Egypt's high level designing information. The accuracy with which monstrous stone blocks were quarried, moved, and put without the utilization of current apparatus keeps on fascinating planners and designers.

Arrangement with Divine Bodies: The pyramids' exact arrangement with the cardinal marks of the compass and their relationship with heavenly bodies like the sun feature the Egyptians' complex galactic comprehension.

Verifiable Importance:

Pharaohs and The great beyond: The pyramids filled in as burial places for pharaohs, reflecting old Egyptian convictions in life following death. The loftiness of these designs represented the pharaoh's heavenly association and status as a ruler.

Solid Record: The Incomparable Pyramid, specifically, held the title of the world's tallest man-made structure for north of 3,800 years, making it one of the most persevering through images of human accomplishment.

Incredible Mass of China

Structural Importance:

Awe-inspiring Scale: The Incomparable Wall's huge length and the utilization of different development materials, including earth, stone, and wood, grandstand China's unrivaled development abilities.

Vital Plan: Lookouts, signal flames, and decisively positioned passes and entryways exhibited the Chinese comprehension of military technique and safeguard.

Verifiable Importance:

Dynastic Safeguard: Worked over hundreds of years, the wall mirrors China's set of experiences of dynastic rule and its techniques to shield against outside dangers from migrant clans.

Worldwide Symbol: Perceived overall as an image of China, the Incomparable Wall remains as a getting through demonstration of the country's solidarity, solidarity, and verifiable versatility.

Machu Picchu, Peru

Compositional Importance:

Dry-Stone Development: Machu Picchu's complicated dry-stone development, without mortar, shows the Inca's high level brick work abilities.

Cosmic Arrangement: Designs like the Intihuatana stone feature the Inca's exact galactic perceptions and arrangement with heavenly occasions.

Verifiable Importance:

Social Retreat: Machu Picchu's stunning area in the midst of the Andes proposes its utilization as an imperial retreat and formal focus, featuring the profound and social meaning of the Inca civilization.

Relinquishment and Rediscovery: Its deserting and resulting rediscovery by Hiram Bingham in 1911 add to its secret and charm.

Acropolis of Athens, Greece

Engineering Importance:

The Parthenon: With its Doric segments and multifaceted friezes, the Parthenon epitomizes traditional Greek engineering's quest for evenness and extent.

Caryatid Segments: The Erechtheion's Caryatid sections feature imaginative and structural advancement.

Verifiable Importance:

Origination of A majority rules system: The Acropolis filled in as a focal social event place for political conversations, making it a notable image of the introduction of a majority rule government.

Social Center point: The Acropolis was a middle for creative, scholarly, and strict pursuits, mirroring the Greeks' love for information, craftsmanship, and otherworldliness.

These famous legacy destinations address design accomplishments as well as windows into the rich embroidery of mankind's set of experiences, convictions, and yearnings. They help us to remember the persevering through tradition of old civilizations and the astounding accomplishments that keep on rousing stunningness and reverence today.

2.7 Preservation challenges and success stories.

Protection Difficulties and Examples of overcoming adversity of Legacy Destinations

Protecting legacy locales presents a perplexing and progressing challenge, yet there have been outstanding examples of overcoming adversity that exhibit the obligation to defending our common social and verifiable fortunes. Notwithstanding, these endeavors are frequently met with different difficulties:

Safeguarding Difficulties:

Regular Rot: Numerous legacy locales are dependent upon normal mileage, including disintegration, enduring, and seismic action. These cycles can cause primary harm over the long haul.

Environmental Change: Climbing temperatures, expanded dampness, and outrageous climate occasions represent a developing danger to legacy locales. Rising ocean levels can likewise imperil seaside locales.

Urbanization: Extending urban areas can infringe upon legacy destinations, causing actual harm and upsetting the general climate.

Contamination: Air contamination, as well as the presence of neighboring enterprises, can prompt ecological debasement and the weakening of memorable materials.

The travel industry Effect: While the travel industry can give imperative income to conservation endeavors, it can likewise prompt congestion, contamination, and harm to delicate designs and relics.

Struggle and Defacement: Equipped contentions, plundering, and defacement have made critical harm legacy destinations in different areas of the planet.

Protection Examples of overcoming adversity:

Angkor Wat, Cambodia: This rambling sanctuary complex confronted dangers from infringing vegetation and defacement. Conservation endeavors, including underlying fixes and guest the executives, have safeguarded this UNESCO World Legacy Site.

Machu Picchu, Peru: Manageable the travel industry rehearses and cautious rebuilding have permitted Machu Picchu to hold its appeal while moderating the effect of guests. Moderates additionally utilize progressed methods to screen and protect the site's underlying uprightness.

The Incomparable Mass of China: Safeguarding endeavors incorporate the reclamation of disintegrating areas, observing for disintegration, and carrying out guest rules to safeguard the wall while permitting dependable the travel industry.

The Acropolis, Greece: The Acropolis went through broad rebuilding work to fix harm brought about by hundreds of years of regular rot, contamination, and past reclamation endeavors. Today, guest numbers are painstakingly figured out how to safeguard the site.

Noteworthy Cairo, Egypt: The memorable focus of Cairo, including milestones like the Ruler Hassan Mosque, confronted dangers from congestion and urbanization. Reclamation endeavors, foundation enhancements, and practical the travel industry drives have safeguarded this UNESCO World Legacy Site.

Venice, Italy: Venice's notorious trenches and memorable structures have confronted dangers from rising ocean levels and mass the travel industry. Safeguarding endeavors incorporate the MOSE task to control flooding and feasible the travel industry missions to oversee guest numbers.

These safeguarding examples of overcoming adversity grandstand the devotion of states, associations, and networks to safeguard our social and verifiable legacy. They act as instances of how cautious preparation, reasonable practices, and global collaboration can guarantee that people in the future can proceed to appreciate and gain from these famous locales. Be that as it may, continuous watchfulness and variation to new difficulties will be fundamental to defending these fortunes for what's to come.

CHAPTER 3

Natural Heritage Wonders

Regular Legacy Marvels: Investigating Earth's Phenomenal Scenes

Normal legacy ponders are the royal gems of our planet, displaying the stunning excellence and amazing powers of nature. These striking scenes, shaped north of millions of years, have spellbound humankind for ages. From the transcending pinnacles of the Himalayas to the profundities of the Excellent Gully, and from the unblemished waters of the Incomparable Boundary Reef to the antiquated backwoods of the Amazon, regular legacy ponders help us to remember the World's significant capacity to make, change, and support life. In this investigation, we will dive into the profundities of a portion of the world's most remarkable normal legacy ponders, revealing their topographical mysteries, environmental importance, and the dire requirement for their safeguarding.

1. **The Incomparable Hindrance Reef, Australia**
   Area: Coral Ocean, off the shore of Queensland, Australia
   Region: North of 344,400 square kilometers
   Topographical and Natural Importance:
   The Incomparable Obstruction Reef is the biggest coral reef framework on The planet and is frequently noticeable from space. It includes large number of individual reefs and islands, making a mosaic of marine environments. Its energetic coral developments, perfectly clear waters, and different marine life make it an UNESCO World Legacy Site and a worldwide fortune.
   Biodiversity Area of interest: The reef is a biodiversity area of interest, home to huge number of types of fish, corals, mollusks, and other marine life. It likewise fills in as a basic living space for various imperiled species, including the dugong and the green ocean turtle.
   Coral Fading: The reef faces dangers from climbing ocean temperatures, sea fermentation, and contamination. Coral fading occasions, set off by

warming waters, have prompted the deficiency of coral cover and undermine the whole environment.

Preservation Endeavors: Preservation drives intend to alleviate the effects of environmental change, diminish contamination, and elevate feasible the travel industry to safeguard the Incomparable Hindrance Reef for people in the future.

2. **The Amazon Rainforest, South America**

   Area: Nine South American nations, essentially Brazil

   Region: Around 5.5 million square kilometers

   Geographical and Environmental Importance:

   The Amazon Rainforest is the biggest tropical rainforest on The planet and covers a tremendous piece of South America. Its rich vegetation, transcending trees, and complex waterway frameworks make a universally huge carbon sink and a support of biodiversity.

   Biodiversity: The Amazon is home to an expected 10% of the world's known species, with innumerable all the more yet to be found. It contains notable natural life like pumas, sloths, and macaws.

   Deforestation: The rainforest faces serious dangers from deforestation, fundamentally determined by logging, agribusiness, and framework improvement. This deficiency of natural surroundings represents a grave gamble to innumerable species and adds to worldwide environmental change.

   Preservation Endeavors: Preservation associations and states are attempting to battle deforestation through safeguarded regions, feasible land-use rehearses, and native land privileges.

3. **The Fantastic Ravine, US**

   Area: Arizona, US

   Length: Roughly 446 kilometers

   Profundity: Up to 1,857 meters

   Topographical and Biological Importance:

   The Fantastic Ravine is a demonstration of the force of disintegration and the boundlessness of geographical time. North of millions of years, the Colorado Stream cut this colossal gap through layers of sedimentary stone, uncovering a geologic record that traverses almost two billion years.

   Topographical History: The gully's stone layers uncover a striking history of Earth's evolving scenes, including times of marine statement, volcanic movement, and structural elevate.

   One of a kind Biological system: The Great Gorge upholds a different exhibit of plant and creature species adjusted to its changed heights and environments. It is home to uncommon and endemic species, like the Fabulous Gorge poisonous snake.

   Challenges: While the Amazing Ravine remains moderately immaculate by direct human turn of events, it faces difficulties from contamination, obtrusive species, and environmental change.

Safeguarding: The Terrific Gorge is safeguarded as a public park, with severe guidelines to protect its regular magnificence and logical worth.

4. **Mount Everest, Nepal and China**
   Area: Himalayas, Nepal, and Tibet Independent District of China
   Level: 8,848.86 meters (29,031.7 feet)
   Topographical and Biological Importance:
   Mount Everest, the world's tallest pinnacle, is an image of both nature's greatness and the persevering assurance of pilgrims and climbers. It is important for the Himalayan mountain range, shaped by the impact of the Indian and Eurasian structural plates.
   Land Arrangement: The Himalayas are as yet ascending because of progressing structural action. Mount Everest itself keeps on becoming taller at a pace of a couple of millimeters every year.
   Outrageous Circumstances: The outrageous height and cruel environment of Everest present huge difficulties to climbers, making it perhaps of the most sought after accomplishment in mountaineering.
   Preservation: Worries about natural effects and congestion on Everest have prompted endeavors to manage getting over licenses and limit the environmental impression on the mountain.

5. **Galápagos Islands, Ecuador**
   Area: Pacific Sea, Ecuador
   Archipelago: 19 islands and various islets
   Topographical and Natural Importance:
   The Galápagos Islands, broadly investigated by Charles Darwin, are a living research facility of development and an UNESCO World Legacy Site.
   Their detachment and extraordinary geography have prompted the advancement of particular and various species found no place else on The planet.
   Natural Variety: The Galápagos are home to various types of turtles, iguanas, birds, and marine life that have adjusted in exceptional ways to their island living spaces.
   Darwin's Hypothesis: Charles Darwin's perceptions in the Galápagos assumed a crucial part in the improvement of his hypothesis of development by regular choice.
   Preservation: Protection endeavors center around shielding the islands' fragile biological systems from obtrusive species, contamination, and overfishing.

6. **Victoria Falls, Zambia and Zimbabwe**
   Area: Zambezi Stream, lining Zambia and Zimbabwe
   Width: Roughly 1,700 meters

Level: Roughly 108 meters

Land and Biological Importance:

Victoria Falls, otherwise called "Mosi-oa-Tunya" (The Smoke That Roars), is one of the world's biggest and most renowned cascades. It is framed by the Zambezi Waterway flowing over an emotional basalt level.

Hydrological Wonder: Victoria Falls is commended for its sheer size and the enormous volume of water that dives into the gap beneath, making a stunning thunder and an unending fog.

Natural Significance: The falls and the encompassing Zambezi Public Park give basic territories to different untamed life, including elephants, hippos, and various bird species.

Preservation: Preservation endeavors expect to safeguard the indigenous habitat and biodiversity of the falls and its environmental elements.

7. **Yosemite Public Park, US**

   Area: California, US

   Region: More than 3,000 square kilometers

   Land and Biological Importance:

   Yosemite Public Park is a demonstration of the force of frosty and erosional powers that have molded its notorious elements, including transcending rock precipices, flowing cascades, and old sequoia trees.

   Stone Developments: Yosemite Valley is famous for its sheer rock bluffs, including El Capitan and Half Vault, which draw in rock climbers and explorers from around the world.

   Cascades: Yosemite is home to various cascades, including Yosemite Falls, North America's tallest cascade, and Bridalveil Fall.

   Biodiversity: The recreation area's different biological systems support a wide exhibit of greenery, including wild bears, donkey deer, and the imperiled Sierra Nevada bighorn sheep.

   Safeguarding: Yosemite Public Park is assigned as an UNESCO World Legacy Site and is safeguarded by the Public Park Administration to guarantee its normal excellence and environmental trustworthiness are saved.

8. **Serengeti Public Park, Tanzania**

   Area: Tanzania

   Region: Roughly 30,000 square kilometers

   Topographical and Natural Importance:

   Serengeti Public Park is inseparable from the quintessential African safari experience. It envelops huge fields, forests, and riverine living spaces, making it quite possibly of the most naturally different district on the mainland.

   Extraordinary Movement: The Serengeti is popular for the yearly Extraordinary Relocation, where a great many wildebeest, zebras, and different herbivores navigate the recreation area looking for crisp touching grounds.

Large Five: The recreation area is home to the "Enormous Five" (lion, panther, elephant, bison, and rhinoceros) and various different species, making it a top objective for untamed life fans.

Protection: Preservation endeavors center around saving the recreation area's extraordinary environments, battling poaching, and guaranteeing practical the travel industry.

9. **Mount Kilimanjaro, Tanzania**
   Area: Tanzania
   Level: 5,895 meters (19,341 feet)
   Geographical and Biological Importance:
   Mount Kilimanjaro is Africa's most noteworthy pinnacle and the world's tallest unsupported mountain. It is a stratovolcano shaped by progressive ejections over centuries.

   Frosty Crown: Kilimanjaro's culmination is delegated by glacial masses and ice fields, regardless of its area close to the equator. These glacial masses are retreating because of environmental change, influencing nearby biological systems and water sources.

   Environmental Zones: The mountain highlights particular natural zones, from rich rainforests at lower heights to elevated deserts and ice sheets close to the culmination.

   Preservation: Preservation endeavors incorporate checking icy retreat and executing reasonable traveling practices to safeguard the mountain's delicate environments.

10. **The Antarctic Promontory, Antarctica**

    Area: Antarctica
    Length: Around 1,300 kilometers
    Geographical and Biological Importance:
    The Antarctic Promontory, the northernmost piece of the Antarctic mainland, is a remote and immaculate wild of ice, icy masses, and mountains. It is home to probably the most outrageous circumstances on The planet and a delicate environment of wonderful versatility.

    Logical Investigation: The promontory has been a point of convergence for logical examination into environmental change, glaciology, and sea life science because of its aversion to an Earth-wide temperature boost.

    Untamed life Overflow: In spite of the cruel climate, the landmass' encompassing waters abound with life, including krill, seals, penguins, and whales.

    Preservation: Peaceful accords, like the Antarctic Deal, are set up to shield this remarkable district from abuse and to advance logical collaboration.

    3.1 Exploration of breathtaking natural heritage sites:

Investigation of Stunning Normal Legacy Locales: An Excursion into Earth's Miracles

Nature's greatness and amazing excellence are on full showcase on the planet's normal legacy locales. These striking areas, painstakingly safeguarded and protected, offer guests an opportunity to observe the World's most dazzling and remarkable scenes. From transcending cascades to old woods and powerful deserts, investigating these destinations is an excursion into the core of our planet's normal marvels.

1. **The Fabulous Gully, US**
   Fabulous Gully
   The Fabulous Gully in Arizona, USA, is a topographical show-stopper that has been etched more than great many years by the Colorado Stream. Traversing 277 miles (446 kilometers) long, up to 18 miles (29 kilometers) in width, and arriving at profundities of more than 1 mile (1.6 kilometers), this amazing abyss grandstands the World's geographical history.
   Investigating the Great Gulch:
   Climbing: The Great Gulch offers various climbing trails, going from simple strolls along the edge to testing backwoods journey that bring you profound into the ravine.
   Boating: Boating down the Colorado Waterway gives an interesting viewpoint of the gulch's transcending bluffs and whitewater rapids.
   Grand Drives: Drive along the South Edge or North Edge to get to perspectives that give all encompassing vistas of the gulch.
2. **The Amazon Rainforest, South America**
   Amazon Rainforest
   The Amazon Rainforest, frequently alluded to as the "lungs of the Earth," is the biggest tropical rainforest on the planet, traversing nine nations in South America. It's a rich, energetic biological system overflowing with different plant and creature life.
   Investigating the Amazon Rainforest:
   Wilderness Trips: Directed wilderness journey bring you profound into the rainforest, where you can experience exceptional natural life and find out about native societies.
   Stream Travels: Investigate the Amazon's streams on a waterway journey, offering chances to recognize pink waterway dolphins, caimans, and lively bird species.
   Shade Strolls: Experience the rainforest from the treetops on overhang walkways, giving an alternate point of view of the thick woodland underneath.
3. **The Incomparable Hindrance Reef, Australia**
   Incredible Hindrance Reef

The Incomparable Boundary Reef off the shoreline of Queensland, Australia, is the world's biggest coral reef framework. This lively submerged wonderland is known for its completely clear waters, brilliant coral developments, and different marine life.

Investigating the Incomparable Boundary Reef:

Swimming and Jumping: Wear your snorkel or scuba stuff to investigate the reef very close, swimming close by a kaleidoscope of fish and perplexing coral nurseries.

Island Bouncing: Visit the different islands and cays inside the Incomparable Hindrance Reef Marine Park for disconnected sea shores and dazzling perspectives.

Glass-Base Boats: In the event that you like to remain dry, take a glass-base boat visit to observe the reef's magnificence from over the waterline.

4. **Machu Picchu, Peru**
   Machu Picchu
   Machu Picchu, settled high in the Andes Heaps of Peru, is an UNESCO World Legacy Site and quite possibly of the most notorious archeological miracle on the planet. This antiquated Incan stronghold is eminent for its complicated dry-stone development and stunning perspectives.

   Investigating Machu Picchu:

   Climbing the Inca Trail: Leave on a multi-day journey along the Inca Trail, coming full circle in a dawn landing in Machu Picchu.

   Train and Transport Visits: Take a grand train excursion to Aguas Calientes, the doorway to Machu Picchu, trailed by a transport ride to the site.

   Directed Visits: Investigate the vestiges with a proficient aide who can give verifiable and social bits of knowledge.

5. **The Galápagos Islands, Ecuador**
   Galápagos Islands
   The Galápagos Islands, situated in the Pacific Sea off the shore of Ecuador, are an extraordinary safe house for untamed life lovers and naturalists. This archipelago is prestigious for its extraordinary biodiversity and its part in Charles Darwin's hypothesis of advancement.

   Investigating the Galápagos Islands:

   Island Bouncing: Visit different islands to observe various types of creatures and extraordinary biological systems.

   Swimming and Scuba Jumping: Plunge into the unmistakable waters to swim with ocean lions, turtles, and brilliant fish.

   Natural life Experiences: Notice monster turtles, marine iguanas, and blue-footed boobies during directed visits.

6. **Victoria Falls, Zambia and Zimbabwe**
   Victoria Falls

Victoria Falls, frequently alluded to as the "smoke that roars," is one of the world's most awesome cascades. It rides the boundary among Zambia and Zimbabwe and is known for its tremendous width and level.

Investigating Victoria Falls:

Perspectives: Various perspectives on the two sides of the falls give dazzling vistas of the flowing waters and the fog that ascents from the crevasse.

Helicopter Flights: Take a helicopter visit for a higher perspective of the falls and the encompassing scenes.

Gutsy Exercises: Experience the excitement of wilderness boating, bungee hopping, or swimming in Satan's Pool, a characteristic stone pool at the edge of the falls.

7. **Yosemite Public Park, US**

   Yosemite Public Park

   Yosemite Public Park in California, USA, is a gold mine of normal magnificence. It's described by transcending stone bluffs, flowing cascades, lavish backwoods, and unblemished glades.

   Investigating Yosemite Public Park:

   Climbing Trails: Yosemite offers a plenty of climbing trails, from simple strolls to testing boondocks courses. Try not to miss the famous Half Vault climb.

   Cascade Touring: Witness the shocking cascades, including Yosemite Falls, Bridalveil Fall, and Vernal Fall.

   Photography: Catch the recreation area's stunning vistas, especially during dawn and dusk.

8. **Serengeti Public Park, Tanzania**

   Serengeti Public Park

   Serengeti Public Park in Tanzania is inseparable from the African safari experience. It is known for its immense savannahs, the yearly Extraordinary Movement, and different natural life.

   Investigating the Serengeti:

   Safari Undertakings: Set out on a safari to detect the "Enormous Five" (lion, panther, elephant, bison, and rhinoceros) and innumerable different creatures.

   Sight-seeing Balloon Rides: Witness the Serengeti from the sky during a critical tourist balloon ride.

   Social Experiences: Investigate the Maasai towns to find out about native societies and customs.

9. **Mount Kilimanjaro, Tanzania**

   Mount Kilimanjaro

   Mount Kilimanjaro is Africa's most noteworthy pinnacle and a lethargic stratovolcano. It's renowned for its snow-covered highest point and its conspicuousness on the Tanzanian scene.

Investigating Mount Kilimanjaro:

Climbing Endeavors: Leave on a provoking trip to the "Top of Africa." Different courses take special care of various expertise levels.

Acclimatization: Permit time for acclimatization as you rise through different natural zones, from rainforests to high deserts.

Uhuru Pinnacle: Stand on the culmination of Uhuru Pinnacle, the most elevated point in Africa, and enjoy all encompassing perspectives.

10. **The Antarctic Landmass, Antarctica**

Antarctic Landmass

The Antarctic Landmass is a remote and unblemished wild at the southernmost tip of the Earth. Its unmistakable scenes, transcending ice shelves, and flourishing natural life make it a novel objective for courageous wayfarers.

Investigating the Antarctic Landmass:

Travels: Join an Antarctic campaign journey to explore frigid waters and land on the mainland, where you can experience penguins, seals, and seabirds.

Logical Exploration: Partake in research campaigns to concentrate on the impacts of environmental change and direct logical examinations in this outrageous climate.

Kayaking and Zodiac Visits: Investigate the landmass' bays and fjords on kayaks or Zodiac boats, furnishing close experiences with untamed life.

3.2 The Galápagos Islands, Ecuador.

The Galápagos Islands, Ecuador: Nature's Living Lab

Settled in the Pacific Sea, around 600 miles (1,000 kilometers) off the shoreline of Ecuador, lies a remote and wonderful archipelago that has caught the creative mind of researchers, travelers, and nature devotees for a really long time — the Galápagos Islands. This group of volcanic islands, framed by topographical powers north of millions of years, has acquired its place as one of the world's most extraordinary and biologically huge objections. Known for its surprising biodiversity and the motivation it gave to Charles Darwin's hypothesis of development, the Galápagos Islands offer a living research facility for the investigation of nature and a safe-haven for a variety of species found no place else on The planet.

Land Starting points

The Galápagos Islands owe their reality to a geographical peculiarity known as area of interest volcanism. The archipelago is arranged on the Nazca Plate, a structural plate in the World's outside layer, where a mantle tuft of liquid stone ascents from profound inside the Earth. As the Nazca Plate moves toward the east over the fixed area of interest, it makes a path of volcanic islands.

The actual islands change in age, with the most seasoned being around 5,000,000 years of age and the most youthful short of what 1,000,000 years of age. Subsequently, they offer a different scope of land highlights, from more seasoned, disintegrated islands with rich high countries to more youthful, more rough islands with ongoing volcanic action.

Special Biodiversity

The Galápagos Islands' confinement and different scope of natural surroundings — going from rich good countries to bone-dry deserts — have led to a mind blowing cluster of verdure. The islands are home to species that have advanced and adjusted to their particular surroundings north of millions of years, bringing about an unrivaled degree of endemism, where creatures are found no place else on The planet.

Notable Types of the Galápagos:

1. **Galápagos Goliath Turtles**
   Galápagos Turtle
   The Galápagos monster turtle is one of the most notorious types of the archipelago. These delicate monsters, some of which can live for more than a long time, have developed into particular subspecies on various islands. Their size and shape fluctuate in view of their island of beginning, reflecting variations to nearby circumstances.

2. **Marine Iguanas**
   The marine iguana is an exceptional animal categories that has adjusted to searching in the sea. It is the main iguana species on the planet that feeds on marine green growth and kelp. Their unmistakable appearance and conduct make them a Galápagos symbol.

3. **Blue-Footed Boobies**
   Blue-footed boobies are known for their striking blue feet, which they use in romance showcases. They are talented trackers, jumping into the sea to get fish and squid. Their populace differs from one island to another.

4. **Galápagos Penguins**
   The Galápagos penguin is one of the world's most extraordinary penguin species and is the main penguin species tracked down north of the equator. They have adjusted to the islands' warm environment and are known for their little size.

5. **Galápagos Ocean Lions**
   Galápagos ocean lions are fun loving and inquisitive animals. They can be spotted relaxing on sea shores, lolling in the sun, or skipping in the water. Their collaborations with guests are a feature of any excursion to the islands.

6. **Galápagos Finches**

The Galápagos finches, frequently alluded to as "Darwin's finches," assumed a critical part in Charles Darwin's hypothesis of development. These birds have adjusted their snout shapes to suit various eating regimens, mirroring their island of beginning.

Darwin's Heritage

The Galápagos Islands hold an extraordinary spot throughout the entire existence of science, especially in the improvement of Charles Darwin's hypothesis of development by normal choice. During his visit to the islands in 1835 on board the HMS Beagle, Darwin mentioned various objective facts and gathered examples that would shape his progressive thoughts.

Darwin's perceptions of the varieties in the mouth states of Galápagos finches, the particular highlights of monster turtles on various islands, and the flexibility of species to their particular surroundings drove him to propose the hypothesis that species develop after some time through a course of regular choice. His work finished in his pivotal book, "On the Beginning of Species," distributed in 1859.

Today, the Galápagos Islands act as a living research center for the investigation of transformative science and biology. Researchers keep on directing exploration on the islands, giving significant bits of knowledge into the components of variation and speciation.

Protection and Difficulties

Notwithstanding their far off area and safeguarded status, the Galápagos Islands face a few protection challenges, basically because of human exercises and intrusive species. These difficulties include:

Intrusive Species

The presentation of non-local species significantly affects the islands' environments. Intrusive species, like rodents, goats, and plants, have disturbed local greenery. Preservation endeavors center around annihilating or controlling these invasives to safeguard the islands' novel biodiversity.

The travel industry

The travel industry, while a crucial wellspring of income for the islands, should be painstakingly figured out how to forestall adverse consequences. Measures incorporate guest standards, assigned guest destinations, and rules to limit unsettling influence to untamed life.

Environmental Change

The Galápagos Islands are not resistant with the impacts of environmental change. Increasing ocean temperatures, sea fermentation, and outrageous climate occasions can hurt marine life and coral reefs. Protectionists are observing these progressions and executing procedures to relieve their effect.

Overfishing

Overfishing can exhaust marine assets and disturb the sensitive equilibrium of the islands' biological systems. Preservation endeavors incorporate maintainable fishing practices and marine stores.

Protection Achievement

Preservation associations, states, and neighborhood networks are working determinedly to safeguard the Galápagos Islands and their remarkable biodiversity. Their endeavors have prompted critical preservation triumphs, including:

Destruction Projects: Effective annihilation programs have disposed of intrusive species like rodents from certain islands, permitting local species to flourish.

Marine Saves: The making of marine holds and safeguarded regions has helped shield the islands' submerged biological systems.

Manageable The travel industry: Guidelines and rules for feasible the travel industry rehearses assist with limiting the ecological effect of guests while giving financial advantages to neighborhood networks.

Logical Exploration: Continuous logical examination gives fundamental information to preservation endeavors and illuminates independent direction.

Guest Experience

Visiting the Galápagos Islands is a rare encounter that offers a significant association with nature and a more profound comprehension of the powers of development. To investigate the islands, guests commonly leave on directed visits that comply to severe protection rules.

Exercises:

Swimming and Jumping: Investigate the submerged world, swimming close by marine life, for example, ocean turtles, sharks, and beams.

Island Jumping: Visit different islands to observe assorted environments and remarkable species.

Untamed life Experiences: Notice the islands' notorious species very close, frequently with the chance to observe interesting and endemic creatures.

Climbing and Investigation: Investigate the islands' volcanic scenes, rich good countries, and immaculate sea shores on directed climbs.

3.3 Serengeti National Park, Tanzania.

Serengeti Public Park, Tanzania: Where the Wild Wanders Indiscriminately

In the core of East Africa, in the midst of the tremendous fields of Tanzania, lies a spot that embodies the untamed substance of the African wild — the Serengeti Public Park. Famous for its general scenes, stunning untamed life, and the display of the Incomparable Relocation, the Serengeti is a demonstration of the getting through magnificence and crude force of nature. It is here that the circle of life works out in the entirety of its greatness, offering a significant and remarkable safari experience.

A Characteristic Show-stopper

The Serengeti, covering roughly 30,000 square kilometers, is Tanzania's leader public park and one of Africa's most celebrated preservation regions. Its name, got from the Maasai language, signifies "Vast Fields," and it satisfies this name, giving a tremendous scope of untainted wild.

Different Environments:

The recreation area's biological systems range from huge lush fields to acacia savannas, riverine timberlands, and rock outcrops known as kopjes. These assorted natural surroundings support a variety of untamed life, each extraordinarily adjusted to its current circumstance.

The Incomparable Relocation

Quite possibly of the most notable regular peculiarity on Earth unfurls in the Serengeti — the Incomparable Movement. Every year, a huge number of wildebeest, zebras, and gazelles embrace an unsafe excursion across the savannas, following the downpours and the lavish grasses that support them. The pattern of relocation is a demonstration of the recreation area's environmental significance.

The Relocation Course:

The relocation follows a clockwise circuit, starting in the southern Serengeti and reaching out into Kenya's Maasai Mara prior to bringing south back. It's a day to day existence and-demise venture, with hunters like lions, cheetahs, and crocodiles anticipating the moving groups.

The Enormous Five and Then some

The Serengeti is prestigious for its amazing cluster of natural life, including the "Enormous Five" (lion, panther, elephant, bison, and rhinoceros). However, the recreation area's biodiversity stretches out a long ways past these notable species.

Famous Natural life:

Lions: The Serengeti brags a flourishing populace lions. They are much of the time spotted relaxing on kopjes or lurking the meadows looking for prey.

Panthers: Slippery and single, panthers possess the recreation area's forests and are a valued sight for untamed life fans.

Elephants: These delicate goliaths are in many cases found close to water sources and give stunning experiences to safari-attendees.

Bison: Enormous crowds of African bison wander the fields, a demonstration of the recreation area's natural wellbeing.

Rhinos: The Serengeti is home to both high contrast rhinoceros, despite the fact that they are more difficult to recognize because of their imperiled status.

Other Untamed life:

Notwithstanding the Enormous Five, the Serengeti abounds with an overflow of untamed life. Cheetahs run across the fields, giraffes smoothly peruse acacia trees, and hippos flounder in quiet hippo pools. The recreation area's birdlife is similarly great, with more than 500 bird species, including vultures, falcons, and vivid transitory birds.

Safari Undertakings

Visiting the Serengeti is a valuable chance to drench yourself in the sights and hints of the African wild. Safari encounters in the recreation area are different and offer something for everybody.

Game Drives:

Game drives are the quintessential Serengeti experience. Talented aides explore the savannas, giving visitors close experiences with untamed life while sharing their insight into the environment's complexities. Dawn and dusk drives offer the best opportunities to detect tricky hunters.

Tourist Balloon Safaris:

For a one of a kind viewpoint, consider a tourist balloon safari. Floating over the Serengeti at first light offers an unmatched perspective on the scenes and untamed life beneath, trailed by a champagne breakfast in the hedge.

Strolling Safaris:

Directed strolling safaris give an opportunity to investigate the more modest miracles of the Serengeti, from following creature impressions to concentrating on the greenery very close. Strolling safaris offer a more profound association with the regular world.

Social Encounters:

Connecting with the Maasai public, who have coincided with the recreation area's untamed life for a really long time, offers a social aspect to your safari. Guests can find out about conventional Maasai ways of life and artworks.

Protection and Difficulties

Saving the Serengeti's immaculate wild and shielding its untamed life is a continuous mission. The recreation area faces a few protection challenges:

Poaching:

Notwithstanding endeavors to battle poaching, the Serengeti stays an objective for unlawful hunting, especially of elephants and rhinoceros. Against poaching drives and local area association are significant in safeguarding these imperiled species.

Living space Misfortune:

Human infringement and animals brushing at the recreation area's boundaries have prompted natural surroundings corruption. Reasonable land-use practices and cradle zones are essential to moderate this issue.

Environmental Change:

The Serengeti isn't insusceptible with the impacts of environmental change. Increasing temperatures and moving precipitation examples can disturb creature movements and influence the accessibility of water and food.

The travel industry Tension:

While the travel industry creates income for preservation endeavors, it likewise puts tension on the recreation area's biological systems. Cautious administration is expected to guarantee that travel industry stays maintainable and limits its effect on natural life.

Protection Achievement

Notwithstanding these difficulties, the Serengeti has seen huge protection victories. Solid associations between government offices, protection associations, and nearby networks have yielded positive outcomes:

Hostile to Poaching Endeavors: Expanded enemy of poaching watches and local area commitment have decreased poaching occurrences.

Natural life Passageways: Drives to make natural life halls and safeguard basic territories have kept up with relocation courses.

Local area Contribution: Including neighborhood networks in preservation endeavors has encouraged a feeling of stewardship and set out financial open doors through the travel industry.

Feasible The travel industry: Severe guidelines and capable the travel industry rehearses guarantee that the recreation area's regular and social legacy is protected.

3.4 Yellowstone National Park, USA.

Yellowstone Public Park, USA: Nature's Wonderland

Settled in the core of the American West, Yellowstone Public Park remains as a demonstration of the wild and untamed excellence of the regular world. Laid out in 1872, it holds the differentiation of being the principal public park on the planet, a title that highlights its importance as a worldwide fortune.

This notorious park, rambling across the territories of Wyoming, Montana, and Idaho, is prestigious for its geothermal marvels, different natural life, and flawless wild. It's where fountains eject, buffalo wander, and guests are drenched in the miracles of the World's land and natural embroidered artwork.

Geographical Wonders

Yellowstone's most striking component is its momentous geothermal scene, a demonstration of the recreation's area on one of the world's biggest dynamic volcanic frameworks. This geographical movement is liable for a heap of normal marvels:

Old Dependable and Fountains

Yellowstone flaunts north of 500 springs, more than elsewhere on The planet. Among them, Old Steadfast stands apart as the recreation area's most popular fascination. It ejects with exceptional consistency, shooting singing water and steam high up in a showcase of nature's accuracy.

Mammoth Natural aquifers

Mammoth Natural aquifers, in the recreation area's northwestern corner, presents a dreamlike scene of travertine porches. These patios are framed by the progression of underground boiling water loaded down with minerals that store as the water arises to the surface. The outcome is a shocking outpouring of white and orange patios, continually developing and reshaping.

Excellent Ravine of the Yellowstone

The Yellowstone Waterway cuts its direction through a profound ravine, making the Terrific Gulch of the Yellowstone. Transcending cascades, for example, Lower Falls and Upper Falls, overflow decisively into the ravine, giving amazing vistas. Craftsman Point is a famous perspective that offers a postcard-ideal perspective on the ravine and falls.

Untamed life Asylum

Yellowstone's different biological systems support a rich embroidery of natural life, making it one of the chief objections for natural life devotees. The recreation area is frequently alluded to as the "Serengeti of North America" because of the overflow and assortment of its creature occupants:

Buffalo

Yellowstone is home to the biggest free-wandering buffalo group on the planet. These famous animals are in many cases seen nibbling on the recreation area's meadows, making an immortal association with the American West's set of experiences.

Wild Bears
Mountain Bear

Yellowstone gives a crucial safe-haven to wild bears. These dominant hunters are an image of wild and can be seen in the recreation area's remote backwoods.

Wolves
Dark Wolf

Wolves, once extirpated from the area, were once again introduced to Yellowstone during the 1990s. Their effective renewed introduction has reestablished harmony to the recreation area's biological systems, making it a head objective for wolf fans.

Elk and Deer

Enormous groups of elk and donkey deer are normally seen all through the recreation area. The pre-winter trench, or mating season, is an ideal time for untamed life lovers to observe these radiant creatures in real life.

Birdlife

Yellowstone's different environments draw in a wide assortment of bird species, including bald eagles, ospreys, trumpeter swans, and the slippery peregrine hawk. Birdwatchers run to the recreation area to notice its avian inhabitants.

Outside Undertakings

Guests to Yellowstone have a plenty of outside exercises to look over, going from comfortable walks around backwoods hiking. Probably the most well known exercises include:

Climbing

The recreation area offers a huge organization of climbing trails that take special care of all expertise levels. Whether you're searching for a short, family-accommodating stroll to a cascade or a multi-day backwoods journey, Yellowstone has everything.

Setting up camp

Yellowstone gives a scope of setting up camp choices, from front-country camping areas with essential conveniences to backwoods setting up camp for those looking for a more vivid encounter. Setting up camp under the stars in the recreation area's wild is a paramount experience.

Untamed life Observing

Noticing untamed life right at home is a feature for some guests. The Lamar Valley and Hayden Valley are known for prime untamed life seeing open doors.

Fishing

The recreation area's lakes, waterways, and streams offer amazing fishing open doors. Fishers can take a shot at local trout species, including ferocious and Yellowstone relentless.

Preservation Difficulties and Triumphs

Saving Yellowstone's novel regular and social legacy is a continuous undertaking. The recreation area faces a few protection challenges, including natural surroundings fracture, obtrusive species, and the effect of environmental change. However, it has accomplished surprising protection victories throughout the long term:

Wolf Renewed introduction: The effective renewed introduction of wolves has prompted better biological systems and more prominent natural equilibrium.

Endorsed Flames: Controlled consumes assist with dealing with the recreation area's vegetation, decrease the gamble of fierce blazes, and reestablish local plant networks.

Wild Bear Recuperation: Yellowstone's mountain bear populace has bounced back, because of defensive measures and environment preservation.

Guest Training: Progressing endeavors to instruct guests about dependable park appearance have prompted more noteworthy mindfulness and stewardship.

3.5 The Great Barrier Reef, Australia.

The Incomparable Obstruction Reef, Australia: Earth's Submerged Wonderland

Underneath the sun-soaked waters of the Coral Ocean, off the northeastern bank of Australia, lies a universe of unmatched excellence and biodiversity — the Incomparable Hindrance Reef. Extending north of 2,300 kilometers (1,430 miles) and containing huge number of coral reefs and islands, this normal miracle is a demonstration of the planet's complicated and delicate environments.

The Incomparable Obstruction Reef isn't simply a coral reef; a living magnum opus of nature has been etched more than great many years, and it holds the title of the biggest living design on The planet.

A Characteristic Wonder

Coral Biological systems

At the core of the Incomparable Boundary Reef are the multifaceted coral environments, worked by minuscule living beings known as coral polyps. These polyps emit calcium carbonate, making immense designs of hard coral. The reef is home to more than 400 types of coral, each adding to the reef's unimaginable variety.

Marine Biodiversity

The reef overflows with marine life, making it one of the world's most assorted environments. It's home to large number of types of fish, mollusks, ocean turtles, and sharks. Famous species like the humpback whale and the bottlenose dolphin incessant the reef's waters.

Vivid Coral

The dynamic shades of the coral are a visual banquet for guests. These tones come from harmonious green growth known as zooxanthellae, which live inside the coral and furnish them with fundamental supplements.

Normal Miracles

The Incomparable Hindrance Reef is studded with normal ponders that leave guests awestruck. The absolute most well known include:

The Incomparable Obstruction Reef Marine Park

The Incomparable Hindrance Reef Marine Park, laid out in 1975, is a tremendous safeguarded region that envelops the reef and its encompassing waters. It's fundamental for the protection and the executives of this amazing biological system.

Heart Reef

Heart Reef is a normally happening coral development that has caught the hearts of sentimental people around the world. It's a famous spot for grand flights and elevated photography.

Whitsunday Islands

The Whitsunday Islands, a piece of the Incomparable Boundary Reef World Legacy Region, are a gathering of 74 islands known for their immaculate sea shores, rich rainforests, and completely clear waters.

The Human Association

The Incomparable Boundary Reef has been occupied by Native Australian people groups for millennia. It holds profound social importance for a few Native gatherings, and their association with the reef is woven into their practices and otherworldliness.

Native Stewardship

Native Association

Native people group in the locale effectively participate in the protection of the reef, mixing conventional information with present day preservation rehearses.

Protection and Difficulties

Notwithstanding its far off area and safeguarded status, the Incomparable Boundary Reef faces various difficulties to its endurance:

Coral Blanching

Increasing ocean temperatures because of environmental change are causing coral fading, an interaction where corals remove their bright green growth, leaving them helpless against sickness and passing.

Sea Fermentation

Expanded degrees of carbon dioxide in the climate are being consumed by the sea, prompting sea fermentation. This makes it challenging for corals to assemble their calcium carbonate skeletons.

Contamination

Overflow from horticultural practices, contamination from beach front turn of events, and marine garbage present critical dangers to the reef's water quality and marine life.

Crown-of-Thistles Starfish

The crown-of-thistles starfish, a characteristic hunter of coral, has seen populace episodes that can decimate coral networks.

Preservation Endeavors

The Australian government, alongside various associations and scientists, is effectively taken part in moderating the Incomparable Boundary Reef. Some key preservation endeavors include:

Decreasing Ozone depleting substance Emanations: Australia is focused on lessening outflows and meeting global environment focuses to moderate the impacts of environmental change on the reef.

Coral Reclamation: Coral rebuilding programs include developing and re-locating versatile coral species to regions impacted by dying and different dangers.

Marine Safeguarded Regions: The Incomparable Obstruction Reef Marine Park Authority has laid out no-take zones and safeguarded regions to save bio-diversity and fish populaces.

Water Quality Improvement: Endeavors are in progress to diminish con-tamination spillover from agribusiness and further develop water quality in reef regions.

Guest Experience

Guests to the Incomparable Boundary Reef have the potential chance to investigate this submerged wonderland through different exercises:

Swimming and Jumping: Swimming and scuba plunging permit guests to get up near the coral, fish, and marine life.

Boat Visits: Directed boat visits give chances to reef investigation and untamed life experiences.

Island Resorts: A few retreats on the reef's islands offer guests an opportunity to unwind and investigate the reef at their own speed.

Instructive Focuses: Interpretive focuses and marine examination stations give experiences into the reef's nature and protection endeavors.

3.6 The ecological importance of each site.

The Environmental Significance of Famous World Legacy Locales

World Legacy Locales are not simply social and regular fortunes; they are likewise essential for the planet's natural wellbeing and manageability. These locales assume a significant part in protecting biodiversity, moderating biological systems, and encouraging a more profound comprehension of our planet's complicated trap of life. We should dive into the biological meaning of some notable World Legacy Destinations.

Serengeti Public Park, Tanzania

Biodiversity Center point: The Serengeti is a foundation of African biodiversity. Its assorted biological systems, from green fields to forests and riverine woodlands, support an amazing exhibit of species, including the "Large Five" (lion, panther, elephant, bison, and rhinoceros). The recreation area is additionally home to endless different warm blooded creatures, birds, and reptiles.

Movement Wonder: The yearly Incredible Relocation, where a large number of wildebeest, zebras, and gazelles cross the Serengeti, is one of the main untamed life displays internationally. This movement supports hunter populaces as well as assists in supplement cycling as creature stays with enhancing the dirt.

Examination and Protection: Researchers and scientists rush to the Serengeti to concentrate on its biological systems and the communications between species. This information illuminates protection endeavors in the recreation area as well as around the world.

The Incomparable Obstruction Reef, Australia

Marine Biodiversity: The Incomparable Boundary Reef is a marine wonderland, lodging north of 1,500 types of fish, 400 types of coral, and various other marine animals. Its rich biodiversity assumes a pivotal part in the soundness of the world's seas.

Coral Reefs and Environment: Coral reefs, similar to those in the Incomparable Obstruction Reef, go about as carbon sinks, engrossing barometrical carbon dioxide and relieving environmental change. Sound reefs likewise safeguard shorelines from disintegration and give a living space to a horde of animal groups.

Logical Center point: The reef fills in as a characteristic lab for sea life scholars and researchers concentrating on environmental change, sea fermentation, and coral dying. These examinations add to how we might interpret worldwide ecological issues.

Yellowstone Public Park, USA

Environment Variety: Yellowstone's shifted biological systems, from geothermal regions to backwoods, knolls, and streams, give natural surroundings to a surprising variety of animal types. Wolves, once missing, were once again introduced to the recreation area, prompting a better and more adjusted environment.

Safeguarding of Jeopardized Species: The recreation area is home to a few imperiled animal groups, like mountain bears, lynx, and dim wolves. Yellowstone assumes an essential part in their protection and recuperation.

Geographical Importance: Yellowstone's geothermal elements, including fountains, underground aquifers, and mud pots, offer significant experiences into Earth's geography and assist researchers with concentrating on volcanic action and warm biological systems.

The Galápagos Islands, Ecuador

Extraordinary Developmental Research facility: The Galápagos Islands are frequently alluded to as a "living lab of advancement" because of their part in moving Charles Darwin's hypothesis of normal determination. They stay an imperative site for the investigation of transformation and speciation.

Exceptional Endemism: The islands are home to species found no place else on The planet, like the Galápagos goliath turtle, marine iguana, and blue-footed booby. Safeguarding these endemic species is fundamental for worldwide biodiversity.

Maritime and Earthbound Variety: The Galápagos support a rich variety of marine life, from penguins and sharks to the ocean lions and marine turtles. Their earthly biological systems likewise have interesting greenery.

The Pyramids of Giza, Egypt

Social Scene: While the Pyramids are principally known for their authentic and social importance, the encompassing desert scene has environmental significance. The desert's bone-dry biological systems are home to adjusted widely varied vegetation, including reptiles and desert foxes.

Biodiversity Desert spring: The Nile Stream, which streams close to the Pyramids, gives an essential wellspring of water and supports different biological systems along its banks. These environments are home to different bird species and backing amphibian life.

Machu Picchu, Peru

Biodiversity Area of interest: The Machu Picchu Memorable Asylum, enveloping the Inca bastion, is situated in the Andes and flaunts astounding biodiversity. The area upholds different vegetation, fauna, and bird species.

Protection and Exploration: The safe-haven assumes a part in preservation endeavors for jeopardized species like the Andean bear and the Andean chicken of-the-rock. Research in this space adds to how we might interpret high-elevation biological systems.

The Acropolis of Athens, Greece

Metropolitan Biodiversity: The Acropolis is a metropolitan World Legacy Site, and its environmental factors offer a brief look into the concurrence of old history and metropolitan biodiversity. The green spaces and archeological destinations have different plants, birds, and bugs.

Authentic Biology: The old Athenians worshipped nature, and their convictions are reflected in the Acropolis' plan and environmental elements. Concentrating on these authentic associations can give experiences into old biological information.

3.7 Conservation efforts and environmental challenges.

The Environmental Significance of Famous World Legacy Locales

World Legacy Locales are not simply social and regular fortunes; they are likewise essential for the planet's natural wellbeing and manageability. These locales assume a significant part in protecting biodiversity, moderating biological systems, and encouraging a more profound comprehension of our planet's complicated trap of life. We should dive into the biological meaning of some notable World Legacy Destinations.

Serengeti Public Park, Tanzania

Biodiversity Center point: The Serengeti is a foundation of African biodiversity. Its assorted biological systems, from green fields to forests and riverine woodlands, support an amazing exhibit of species, including the "Large Five" (lion, panther, elephant, bison, and rhinoceros). The recreation area is additionally home to endless different warm blooded creatures, birds, and reptiles.

Movement Wonder: The yearly Incredible Relocation, where a large number of wildebeest, zebras, and gazelles cross the Serengeti, is one of the main untamed life displays internationally. This movement supports hunter populaces as well as assists in supplement cycling as creature stays with enhancing the dirt.

Examination and Protection: Researchers and scientists rush to the Serengeti to concentrate on its biological systems and the communications between species. This information illuminates protection endeavors in the recreation area as well as around the world.

The Incomparable Obstruction Reef, Australia

Marine Biodiversity: The Incomparable Boundary Reef is a marine wonderland, lodging north of 1,500 types of fish, 400 types of coral, and various other marine animals. Its rich biodiversity assumes a pivotal part in the soundness of the world's seas.

Coral Reefs and Environment: Coral reefs, similar to those in the Incomparable Obstruction Reef, go about as carbon sinks, engrossing barometrical carbon dioxide and relieving environmental change. Sound reefs likewise safeguard shorelines from disintegration and give a living space to a horde of animal groups.

Logical Center point: The reef fills in as a characteristic lab for sea life scholars and researchers concentrating on environmental change, sea fermentation, and coral dying. These examinations add to how we might interpret worldwide ecological issues.

Yellowstone Public Park, USA

Environment Variety: Yellowstone's shifted biological systems, from geothermal regions to backwoods, knolls, and streams, give natural surroundings to a surprising variety of animal types. Wolves, once missing, were once again introduced to the recreation area, prompting a better and more adjusted environment.

Safeguarding of Jeopardized Species: The recreation area is home to a few imperiled animal groups, like mountain bears, lynx, and dim wolves. Yellowstone assumes an essential part in their protection and recuperation.

Geographical Importance: Yellowstone's geothermal elements, including fountains, underground aquifers, and mud pots, offer significant experiences into Earth's geography and assist researchers with concentrating on volcanic action and warm biological systems.

The Galápagos Islands, Ecuador

Extraordinary Developmental Research facility: The Galápagos Islands are frequently alluded to as a "living lab of advancement" because of their part in moving Charles Darwin's hypothesis of normal determination. They stay an imperative site for the investigation of transformation and speciation.

Exceptional Endemism: The islands are home to species found no place else on The planet, like the Galápagos goliath turtle, marine iguana, and blue-footed booby. Safeguarding these endemic species is fundamental for worldwide biodiversity.

Maritime and Earthbound Variety: The Galápagos support a rich variety of marine life, from penguins and sharks to the ocean lions and marine turtles. Their earthly biological systems likewise have interesting greenery.

The Pyramids of Giza, Egypt

Social Scene: While the Pyramids are principally known for their authentic and social importance, the encompassing desert scene has environmental significance. The desert's bone-dry biological systems are home to adjusted widely varied vegetation, including reptiles and desert foxes.

Biodiversity Desert spring: The Nile Stream, which streams close to the Pyramids, gives an essential wellspring of water and supports different biological systems along its banks. These environments are home to different bird species and backing amphibian life.

Machu Picchu, Peru

Biodiversity Area of interest: The Machu Picchu Memorable Asylum, enveloping the Inca bastion, is situated in the Andes and flaunts astounding biodiversity. The area upholds different vegetation, fauna, and bird species.

Protection and Exploration: The safe-haven assumes a part in preservation endeavors for jeopardized species like the Andean bear and the Andean chicken of-the-rock. Research in this space adds to how we might interpret high-elevation biological systems.

The Acropolis of Athens, Greece

Metropolitan Biodiversity: The Acropolis is a metropolitan World Legacy Site, and its environmental factors offer a brief look into the concurrence of old history and metropolitan biodiversity. The green spaces and archeological destinations have different plants, birds, and bugs.

Authentic Biology: The old Athenians worshipped nature, and their convictions are reflected in the Acropolis' plan and environmental elements. Concentrating on these authentic associations can give experiences into old biological information.

CHAPTER 4

The UNESCO World Heritage Process

The UNESCO World Legacy Cycle: Protecting Mankind's Fortunes

The UNESCO World Legacy process is an exceptional undertaking that means to recognize, safeguard, and commend spots of remarkable social, regular, and verifiable importance all over the planet. It is a demonstration of mankind's aggregate obligation to saving our planet's most valued treasures for current and people in the future. In this extensive investigation, we'll travel through the many-sided and motivating cycle that prompts the assignment of a World Legacy Site.

Grasping World Legacy

The idea of World Legacy rose up out of the acknowledgment that specific puts on Earth have exceptional worth and importance to all of mankind, rising above public limits. These spots are not only images of our common history and culture yet additionally archives of indispensable biodiversity and regular marvels. To protect and advance these exceptional destinations, UNESCO (the Unified Countries Instructive, Logical and Social Association) laid out the World Legacy program in 1972.

Measures for World Legacy

Before a site can be assigned as a World Legacy Site, it should meet explicit measures. There are ten standards altogether, isolated into three classes: social, regular, and blended (destinations that have both social and normal worth). Here is a more intensive glance at these standards:

Social Rules

Standard (I): Address a magnum opus of human imaginative virtuoso: Destinations that display excellent human innovativeness, for example, engineering wonders like the Pyramids of Giza or creative accomplishments like the works of art in the Lascaux Caverns.

Model (ii): Display a significant exchange of human qualities: Locales that give testimony regarding huge social connections, for example, shipping lanes like the Silk Street or exchanging settlements like the Noteworthy Focus of Florence.

Measure (iii): Give a special or if nothing else uncommon declaration to a social custom or human progress: Destinations that offer bits of knowledge into evaporated or as yet flourishing societies, like the memorable towns of Ouro Preto (Brazil) or Bhaktapur (Nepal).

Measure (iv): Be a remarkable illustration of a sort of building, engineering, or mechanical group, or scene that represents a critical stage in mankind's set of experiences: Locales that exhibit design ability, similar to the noteworthy focus of Rome, or mechanical headways, similar to the Ironbridge Canyon in the UK.

Standard (v): Be a remarkable illustration of a customary human settlement, land use, or ocean use which is illustrative of a culture (or societies), or human connection with the climate: Locales that reflect conventional lifestyles and amicable concurrence with nature, like the Laponian Region in Sweden.

Regular Standards

Basis (vii): Contain standout regular peculiarities or areas of uncommon normal excellence and stylish significance: Locales that brag stunning scenes or novel regular peculiarities, similar to the Incomparable Boundary Reef in Australia or the Goliath's Highway in Northern Ireland.

Model (viii): Be exceptional models addressing significant phases of Earth's set of experiences, including the record of life, huge continuous geographical cycles in the improvement of landforms, or critical geomorphic or physiographic highlights: Locales that uncover Earth's topographical history, similar to the Iguazu Public Park in Argentina or the Galápagos Islands in Ecuador.

Basis (ix): Be exceptional models addressing huge continuous environmental and organic cycles in the advancement and improvement of earthbound, freshwater, seaside, and marine biological systems and networks of plants and creatures: Locales that are focal points of biodiversity and normal cycles, for example, the Sundarbans mangrove timberland in Bangladesh.

Blended Measures

Measure (x): Contain the most significant and huge normal living spaces for in-situ protection of natural variety, including those containing undermined types of exceptional widespread worth according to the perspective of science or preservation: Destinations that are both socially and normally critical, as Machu Picchu in Peru or Mount Athos in Greece.

Model (vi): Be straightforwardly or unmistakably connected with occasions or residing customs, with thoughts, or with convictions, with imaginative and abstract works of exceptional general importance: Destinations that have both social and normal worth, like the Mount Athos in Greece, where religious practices coincide with special regular scenes.

Selecting a Site

The way to World Legacy assignment starts with a country's administration selecting a site inside its nation for thought. This selection is ordinarily an intricate and careful interaction that includes broad examination, documentation, and conference with nearby networks and partners.

Speculative Rundown

Before formally choosing a site, nations frequently put it on their "provisional rundown." This rundown fills in as a primer stock of locales that the nation accepts have World Legacy potential. It gives a chance to evaluate the site's reasonableness, accumulate fundamental information, and set up a vigorous designation.

Setting up the Designation

When a site is chosen for designation, the country's administration should set up an extensive selection dossier. This dossier, directed by UNESCO's severe rules, should give nitty gritty data on the site's importance, the executives, and protection plans. It ought to likewise incorporate guides, photos, and some other significant documentation.

Warning Bodies

After accommodation, the selection goes through a thorough assessment process. UNESCO depends on three warning bodies to evaluate assignments: the Global Chamber on Landmarks and Destinations (ICOMOS) for social locales, the Worldwide Association for Protection of Nature (IUCN) for regular locales, and the Worldwide Place for the Investigation of the Conservation and Rebuilding of Social Property (ICCROM) for both social and blended destinations.

These warning bodies assess the assignments in light of the measures referenced before. They additionally consider factors like administration plans, lawful assurance, and the site's trustworthiness and legitimacy. Their assessments give proposals to the World Legacy Board of trustees.

World Legacy Advisory group

The World Legacy Board is made out of agents from 21 part states chose by the Overall Get together of States Gatherings for the World Legacy Show. This panel meets yearly to survey and support assignments.

Assessment and Choice

During the board of trustees' meetings, every assignment is introduced, and the warning bodies' assessments are examined. The panel might demand extra data, look for explanation, or make changes to the designations. Eventually, they conclude whether a site ought to be recorded as a World Legacy Site or not.

Engraving and Observing

In the event that a site is supported, it is officially engraved on the World Legacy Rundown. This assignment perceives the site's extraordinary all inclusive worth and triggers global responsibilities to its security and conservation. Nonetheless, it additionally accompanies liabilities. The nation should carry out powerful administration and preservation plans, consistently report on the site's status, and go to restorative lengths if essential.

Protection and Difficulties

When a site is assigned as a World Legacy Site, crafted by defending its excellent worth starts. Protection endeavors can take different structures, contingent upon the site's inclination and difficulties:

Social Legacy Protection

Rebuilding and Protection: For authentic destinations and landmarks, protection frequently includes cautious reclamation and conservation to keep up with their unique appearance and trustworthiness.

Documentation and Exploration: Progressing research uncovers stowed away parts of social legacy and illuminate preservation rehearses.

Local area Commitment: Connecting with neighborhood networks is imperative to guarantee that protection endeavors regard social practices and cultivate a feeling of pride.

Regular Legacy Protection

Territory Assurance: For regular destinations, the essential center is natural surroundings insurance, frequently through the foundation of safeguarded regions and untamed life passages.

Hostile to Poaching Measures: Forestalling unlawful poaching and exchange jeopardized species is a vital part of protection.

Environment Flexibility: Given the rising dangers of environmental change, systems to upgrade the versatility of regular destinations are acquiring significance.

Challenges

While the World Legacy process has made exceptional progress in safeguarding our planet's fortunes, it faces a few difficulties:

Environmental Change

Increasing temperatures, ocean level ascent, and outrageous climate occasions compromise both social and regular World Legacy Locales. Notorious spots like Venice and the Incomparable Obstruction Reef are in danger.

Over-The travel industry

Famous World Legacy Locales frequently face over-the travel industry, which can prompt natural debasement, congestion, and harm to social legacy.

Struggle and Obliteration

Outfitted clashes and conscious demonstrations of obliteration present huge dangers to World Legacy Locales, as found in Syria and Iraq.

Deficient Assets

Numerous nations miss the mark on assets and skill to successfully oversee and safeguard their Reality Legacy Locales.

Adjusting Protection and Improvement

Offsetting protection with the monetary necessities of neighborhood networks can be testing, especially in emerging nations.

Examples of overcoming adversity

Notwithstanding these difficulties, the World Legacy process has commended various victories. Remarkable models include:

The recuperation of the dim wolf populace in Yellowstone Public Park after renewed introduction.

The reclamation of Venice's memorable structures through the "MoSE" project.

The security of the Virunga Public Park in the Majority rule Republic of Congo, home to jeopardized mountain gorillas.

The cooperative work to ration the histo

4.1 Detailed explanation of the nomination and inscription process.

The UNESCO World Legacy Assignment and Engraving Interaction: Protecting Our Worldwide Fortunes

The UNESCO World Legacy designation and engraving process is a careful and thorough excursion that comes full circle in the acknowledgment and security of extraordinary social, regular, and blended legacy destinations all over the planet. This cycle, represented by the World Legacy Show embraced in 1972, includes a progression of steps, assessments, and choices that eventually lead to the engraving of a site on the esteemed World Legacy Rundown.

The Way to World Legacy Assignment

Stage 1: Speculative Rundown

The excursion to World Legacy status frequently starts with a country's production of a "speculative rundown." This rundown involves likely destinations inside the nation's boundaries that have excellent social, normal, or blended esteem. The incorporation of a site on the conditional rundown is an underlying step towards possible selection. It permits nations to survey the reasonableness of locales, accumulate fundamental information, and draw in partners simultaneously.

Stage 2: Setting up the Designation

When a site is chosen for selection, the country's administration sets out on a thorough excursion of examination, documentation, and planning. The designation dossier, a critical part of this step, should comply to UNESCO's thorough rules and give a point by point record of the site's importance, the board, and protection plans. It ought to likewise incorporate guides, photos, and some other pertinent documentation.

Stage 3: Counsel and Partner Commitment

A basic part of the designation cycle is meeting and partner commitment. Nearby people group, native gatherings, and different partners with a personal stake in the site are counseled to guarantee that their points of view and concerns are considered. This comprehensive methodology adds to the improvement of a balanced selection dossier.

Stage 4: Assessment by Warning Bodies

With the assignment dossier close by, the nation presents its selection to UNESCO. The assessment cycle is directed by three critical warning bodies:

Worldwide Gathering on Landmarks and Destinations (ICOMOS):

ICOMOS surveys social destinations, assessing their verifiable, building, and social importance. Specialists from ICOMOS lead nearby visits and give definite reports and suggestions.

Worldwide Association for Protection of Nature (IUCN):

IUCN assesses normal destinations, taking into account their biological worth, biodiversity, and preservation status. Like ICOMOS, specialists from IUCN lead nearby assessments and give reports and suggestions.

Worldwide Community for the Investigation of the Conservation and Reclamation of Social Property (ICCROM):

ICCROM assumes a part in surveying both social and blended destinations. While not so often involved as ICOMOS and IUCN, ICCROM's ability in protection and reclamation is significant.

These warning bodies thoroughly assess designations in view of UNESCO's rules for social, regular, or blended legacy destinations.

Stage 5: The World Legacy Board of trustees

The World Legacy Board of trustees, made out of delegates from 21 part states chose by the Overall Gathering of States Gatherings for the World Legacy Show, assembles yearly to survey and settle on the designations.

Assessment and Choice:

During the board of trustees' meetings, every selection is introduced, and the warning bodies' assessments are examined. The board might demand extra data, look for explanation, or make alterations to the assignments. Eventually, they conclude whether a site ought to be recorded as a World Legacy Site or not.

Deferral and Reference:

At times, the board might concede a choice, normally mentioning extra data or further assessments. A reference happens when a selection is considered inadequate or deficient for engraving, requiring the country to resubmit the designation with modifications.

Stage 6: Engraving

On the off chance that a site is endorsed by the World Legacy Panel, it is officially recorded on the World Legacy Rundown. This assignment perceives the site's exceptional widespread worth and involves global responsibilities to its insurance and safeguarding. Engraving fills in as a renowned characteristic of acknowledgment, praising a site's importance on the worldwide stage.

The Significance of World Legacy Engraving

Worldwide Acknowledgment

World Legacy engraving carries worldwide acknowledgment to a site's excellent worth. It connotes that a site has extraordinary all inclusive importance, rising above public limits.

Obligation to Safeguarding

With World Legacy status comes a promise to saving the site for current and people in the future. This incorporates the execution of viable administration and protection plans, normal investigating the site's status, and going to restorative lengths if essential.

Worldwide Participation

World Legacy engraving encourages global participation. It frequently includes coordinated effort between nations, associations, and specialists to defend the site.

Instructive and Social Worth

World Legacy Destinations offer instructive and social worth. They give chances to research, the travel industry, and social trade, enhancing how we might interpret the world's different legacy.

Difficulties and Obligations

While the World Legacy process has commended various triumphs in safeguarding worldwide fortunes, it likewise faces huge difficulties:

Environmental Change

Climbing temperatures, ocean level ascent, and outrageous climate occasions compromise both social and normal World Legacy Destinations. Notorious spots like Venice and the Incomparable Obstruction Reef are in danger.

Over-The travel industry

Well known World Legacy Locales frequently face over-the travel industry, which can prompt ecological corruption, congestion, and harm to social legacy.

Struggle and Annihilation

Equipped struggles and conscious demonstrations of obliteration present huge dangers to World Legacy Locales, as found in Syria and Iraq.

Lacking Assets

Numerous nations come up short on assets and ability to really oversee and safeguard their Reality Legacy Locales.

Adjusting Protection and Advancement

Offsetting protection with the financial requirements of neighborhood networks can be testing, especially in agricultural nations.

Examples of overcoming adversity

Regardless of these difficulties, the World Legacy process has praised various victories. Prominent models include:

The recuperation of the dark wolf populace in Yellowstone Public Park after renewed introduction.

The rebuilding of Venice's notable structures through the "MoSE" project.

The security of the Virunga Public Park in the Popularity based Republic of Congo, home to jeopardized mountain gorillas.

The cooperative work to monitor the memorable city of Timbuktu in Mali.

4.2 The role of advisory bodies and site management.

The Job of Warning Bodies and Site The board in World Legacy Protection

The protection of World Legacy Locales is a mind boggling and diverse undertaking that includes the cooperative endeavors of different partners, including warning bodies and site the board specialists. These substances assume critical parts in surveying the worth of likely locales, guaranteeing their preservation, and dealing with their continuous security. In this investigation, we will dig into the vital jobs of warning bodies, like ICOMOS and IUCN, and the obligations of site the board in shielding these worldwide fortunes.

The Warning Bodies: ICOMOS and IUCN

ICOMOS (Global Board on Landmarks and Destinations) and IUCN (Global Association for Protection of Nature) are two unmistakable warning bodies endowed with assessing and giving suggestions on designations to World Legacy Locales. Each assumes a specific part founded on the idea of the site — ICOMOS centers around social legacy, while IUCN focuses on regular legacy.

ICOMOS: Defending Social Legacy

ICOMOS is committed to saving and safeguarding social legacy around the world. Its essential obligations inside the World Legacy process include:

Master Assessment: ICOMOS conducts top to bottom appraisals of assigned social locales. Specialists from ICOMOS do nearby visits, assessing the verifiable, design, and social meaning of the locales.

Credibility and Respectability: ICOMOS assesses the legitimacy and trustworthiness of social destinations. Credibility alludes to the site's capacity to convey its social worth honestly, while respectability relates to the site's flawlessness and completeness.

The executives Plans: ICOMOS audits the administration plans proposed by site the board specialists to guarantee they are satisfactory for defending the site's qualities.

Suggestions: In light of its assessments, ICOMOS gives proposals to the World Legacy Board of trustees. These suggestions might incorporate writing a site on the World Legacy Rundown, conceding a choice for additional assessment, or alluding the designation back to the country for modifications.

Protection Mastery: ICOMOS offers skill in preservation practices, rebuilding, and conservation strategies, helping site the board experts in keeping up with and defending social legacy.

IUCN: Moderating Normal Legacy

IUCN is devoted to the protection of nature and biodiversity. Its essential obligations inside the World Legacy process include:

Assessing Normal Locales: IUCN assesses named regular destinations, zeroing in on their environmental worth, biodiversity, and preservation status. Specialists from IUCN direct nearby assessments and appraisals.

Biological Importance: IUCN evaluates the environmental meaning of normal destinations, taking into account their part in saving basic living spaces, species, and regular cycles.

Dangers and Preservation: IUCN recognizes dangers to normal locales, for example, living space annihilation, environmental change, and poaching, and assesses the viability of protection measures proposed by site the board specialists.

Suggestions: Like ICOMOS, IUCN gives proposals to the World Legacy Board of trustees in light of its assessments. These suggestions can incorporate engraving, deferral, or reference for additional consideration.

Biodiversity Preservation: IUCN's ability reaches out to systems for moderating biodiversity and overseeing environments, helping site the executives experts in their protection endeavors.

Site The executives Specialists: The Watchmen of World Legacy

Site the executives specialists, frequently at the public or neighborhood level, act as the watchmen of World Legacy Destinations. They are liable for the everyday administration, security, and preservation of these significant spots. Their jobs and obligations are broad and envelop a scope of exercises.

Creating The board Plans

One of the essential obligations of site the executives specialists is the advancement of exhaustive administration plans. These plans frame methodologies for the conservation of the site's social, normal, or blended values. They address issues, for example, guest the board, preservation works on, observing of dangers, and practical the travel industry.

Carrying out Protection Measures

Site the executives specialists are entrusted with carrying out preservation estimates that guarantee the site's honesty and realness. This can include rebuilding work, natural surroundings assurance, the conservation of social antiquities, and the upkeep of environmental equilibrium. They team up with specialists and partners to do these exercises.

Observing and Revealing

Nonstop observing of the site's condition is fundamental. Site the executives specialists gather information on ecological and social pointers to survey the site's wellbeing and address arising dangers. They report consistently to UNESCO on the condition of preservation, including victories and difficulties confronted.

Connecting with Neighborhood People group

Nearby people group frequently have a profound association with World Legacy Locales. Site the board specialists draw in with these networks to cultivate a feeling of responsibility and guarantee that preservation endeavors regard neighborhood customs and information. Local area association can go from business open doors to social protection drives.

Adjusting The travel industry and Protection

World Legacy Destinations frequently draw in travelers, adding to nearby economies. Site the executives specialists face the test of adjusting the advantages of the travel industry with the requirement for site safeguarding. Feasible the travel industry rehearses that limit ecological effect and regard social qualities are critical.

Answering Dangers

Site the executives specialists should answer quickly to dangers, for example, cataclysmic events, environmental change influences, and criminal operations. They foster crisis plans and systems to alleviate possible harm and recuperate from unfavorable occasions.

Looking for Global Help

In situations where a site faces critical difficulties past the assets of the host country, site the executives specialists might look for worldwide help and co-operation. This can include associations with associations, financing help, and specialized aptitude.

Difficulties and Obligations

Protecting and overseeing World Legacy Locales isn't without challenges. Site the executives specialists face a scope of issues, including:

Asset Imperatives

Many site the executives specialists work with restricted assets, making it trying to carry out far reaching protection and the board designs really.

Over-The travel industry

Famous World Legacy Destinations frequently experience over-the travel industry, prompting stuffing, ecological debasement, and tension on nearby networks.

Environmental Change

The effects of environmental change, including increasing temperatures, ocean level ascent, and outrageous climate occasions, compromise the trust-worthiness of both social and normal legacy destinations.

Struggle and Annihilation

Equipped contentions and demonstrations of annihilation can present prompt and serious dangers to World Legacy Destinations, as found in areas like Syria and Iraq.

Adjusting Protection and Advancement

Dealing with the sensitive harmony between preserving World Legacy Destinations and meeting the monetary necessities of nearby networks can be a mind boggling and continuous test.

Examples of overcoming adversity

Notwithstanding these difficulties, various victories feature the adequacy of site the board and global cooperation. A few prominent accomplishments include:

The recuperation of the dark wolf populace in Yellowstone Public Park after effective renewed introduction endeavors.

The reclamation and protection of memorable structures in Venice through projects like the "MoSE" framework.

The security and protection of the Virunga Public Park in the Vote based Republic of Congo, home to imperiled mountain gorillas.

The cooperative endeavors to ration the memorable city of Timbuktu in Mali, defending its social fortunes.

4.3 How communities and countries benefit from World Heritage status. How People group and Nations Advantage from World Legacy Status

World Legacy status, granted by UNESCO (the Unified Countries Instructive, Logical and Social Association), addresses worldwide acknowledgment of a site's remarkable widespread worth. This lofty assignment not just commends the social, regular, or blended legacy of a specific spot yet in addition carries a great many advantages to both the nearby networks and the nations in which these locales are found. In this investigation, we will dig into the bunch manners by which networks and nations receive the benefits of World Legacy status.

Protecting Social and Normal Heritages

At the core of World Legacy status lies the protection of social and normal fortunes. These destinations are frequently of massive verifiable, creative, or biological worth. By writing a site on the World Legacy Rundown, people group and nations focus on defending their rich heritages for current and people in the future.

1. **Social Character and Pride:** World Legacy Destinations are a wellspring of social personality and pride for neighborhood networks and countries. They represent the accomplishments, customs, and legacy of a group. This acknowledgment encourages a feeling of having a place and shared social personality.

2. **Social Trade and Understanding:** World Legacy Destinations draw in global guests, advancing social trade and understanding. This communication between assorted societies can prompt expanded resilience, appreciation, and familiarity with worldwide variety.

3. **Financial Advantages:** The travel industry to World Legacy Destinations frequently drives monetary development in nearby networks. Guests burn through cash on facilities, food, gifts, and directed visits, adding to the nearby economy and setting out work open doors.

Practical The travel industry

World Legacy status supports maintainable the travel industry works on, guaranteeing that the monetary advantages of the travel industry don't come to the detriment of the site's respectability and the prosperity of nearby networks.

1. **Guest The executives:** UNESCO supports dependable and controlled appearance to World Legacy Destinations. Site the executives specialists carry out procedures to limit the natural effect of the travel industry and safeguard delicate biological systems.
2. **Pay Expansion:** The income created from the travel industry can be re-invested in the protection and the board of the site. This monetary help keeps up with the site's realness and shields it from commercialization.
3. **Social Safeguarding:** Maintainable the travel industry frequently incorporates drives to protect and exhibit neighborhood social customs, painstaking work, and customary practices. This gives an extra kind of revenue for nearby networks.

Schooling and Exploration

World Legacy Locales act as living homerooms and examination labs, offering instructive and logical open doors to networks and nations.

1. **Instructive Projects:** Numerous World Legacy Destinations have instructive projects for schools and colleges, permitting understudies to find out about history, culture, and the climate through direct encounters.
2. **Logical Exploration:** Analysts and researchers are attracted to World Legacy Locales to concentrate on their remarkable biological systems, social practices, and verifiable importance. This exploration adds to how we might interpret different fields, from antiquarianism to environment.
3. **Conservation Mastery:** The aptitude expected for the safeguarding and rebuilding of World Legacy Destinations frequently prompts the advancement of particular abilities and information inside nearby networks and nations.

Global Joint effort and Acknowledgment

World Legacy Locales benefit from global cooperation and backing, upgrading their conservation endeavors.

1. **Specialized Help:** UNESCO gives specialized help, skill, and financing to nations and networks to help the protection and the board of World Legacy Destinations.

2. **Cooperative Undertakings:** Global associations and state run administrations might team up on projects pointed toward saving and advancing World Legacy Destinations, prompting improved preservation endeavors and site the executives.

3. **Worldwide Acknowledgment:** World Legacy status lifts a site to worldwide noticeable quality. It is much of the time highlighted in global media, narratives, and instructive materials, expanding its perceivability and acknowledgment on the world stage.

Fortifying Social Discretion

World Legacy Locales have the ability to fortify social discretion by cultivating participation and discourse among countries.

1. **Social Tact:** Nations with World Legacy Locales frequently participate in social discretion by advancing their destinations as images of harmony, legacy, and shared mankind. This can prompt positive worldwide relations and joint efforts.

2. **Cross-Boundary Coordinated effort:** Transnational World Legacy Locales, which length numerous nations, empower participation and tact among countries. These locales feature the interconnectedness of worldwide legacy.

Difficulties and Obligations

While the advantages of World Legacy status are significant, they accompany critical obligations and difficulties:

1. **Preservation Commitments:** Nations and networks should focus on the protection and assurance of the site, which can include huge interests in assets and ability.

2. **Adjusting Improvement:** Finding some kind of harmony between monetary turn of events and site conservation is frequently difficult. Maintainable advancement plans should be painstakingly created to safeguard the site's honesty.

3. **Over-The travel industry:** Dealing with the deluge of sightseers to famous World Legacy Locales can be troublesome. Over-the travel industry can prompt congestion, natural debasement, and burden on nearby assets.

4. **Environmental Change:** World Legacy Locales are progressively defenseless against the impacts of environmental change, including increasing temperatures, ocean level ascent, and outrageous climate occasions. Sufficient measures should be taken to alleviate these dangers.

5. **Struggle and Security:** Destinations in locales of contention might confront quick dangers to their conservation. Guaranteeing the wellbeing and security of these destinations is principal.

Examples of overcoming adversity

Regardless of these difficulties, various examples of overcoming adversity exhibit the positive effects of World Legacy status:

The supportable the travel industry rehearses in Machu Picchu, Peru, have protected this notable site while helping the nearby local area monetarily.

The Serengeti Public Park in Tanzania has turned into a main illustration of compelling untamed life protection and local area commitment.

The assurance and protection endeavors at Angkor Wat in Cambodia have reestablished this antiquated sanctuary complex to its previous brilliance, drawing in great many guests yearly.

CHAPTER 5

Challenges and Threats

Difficulties and Dangers to World Legacy Destinations
World Legacy Destinations, regardless of their extraordinary general worth, are not safe to a large number of difficulties and dangers that imperil their conservation and honesty. These dangers emerge from different sources, including regular cycles, human exercises, and international elements. In this exhaustive investigation, we will dig into the horde difficulties and dangers that World Legacy Destinations face and their expected outcomes.
Normal Difficulties and Dangers

1. **Environmental Change:** Environmental change presents one of the main dangers to World Legacy Locales. Climbing temperatures, ocean level ascent, expanded recurrence of outrageous climate occasions, and adjusted precipitation examples can prompt territory misfortune, disintegration, and the debasement of social landmarks.
2. **Cataclysmic events:** Tremors, volcanic ejections, waves, and tropical storms can bring about quick and devastating harm to World Legacy Locales. Such occasions can obliterate social legacy and disturb delicate environments.
3. **Disintegration:** Beach front and inland disintegration can gradually dissolve social designs and regular scenes. Beach front locales, specifically, are defenseless against ocean level ascent and disintegration.
4. **Illness and Vermin:** Episodes of sicknesses and obtrusive species can affect both normal and social World Legacy Locales. For instance, sicknesses influencing coral reefs, similar to coral dying, can crush marine environments.
5. **Out of control fires:** Fierce blazes can undermine both normal and social legacy. They can annihilate verifiable structures, curios, and indispensable

environments.

Human-Initiated Difficulties and Dangers

6. **Over-The travel industry:** The flood of sightseers can prompt congestion, natural debasement, and harm to social legacy. Over-the travel industry strains neighborhood assets and foundation.

7. **Improvement Strain:** Urbanization, foundation projects, and unregulated advancement can infringe upon World Legacy Destinations, adjusting their scenes and compromising their legitimacy.

8. **Contamination:** Contamination from ventures, horticulture, and metropolitan regions can hurt both normal and social legacy. Air and water contamination can consume memorable designs and mischief environments.

9. **Deforestation:** Deforestation and living space misfortune can essentially affect regular World Legacy Locales. Loss of living space can prompt species elimination and disturb environments.

10. **Criminal operations:** Poaching, unlawful logging, and plundering of social curios present critical dangers. These exercises can exhaust biodiversity and deny the universe of social fortunes.

International Difficulties and Dangers

11. **Furnished Struggle:** World Legacy Destinations situated in districts of equipped clash face prompt and extreme dangers. They can be harmed or obliterated deliberately as a feature of military activities.

12. **Common Agitation:** Common distress and political shakiness can disturb the administration and security of World Legacy Destinations, making them powerless against plundering and harm.

13. **Line Questions:** Transnational World Legacy Destinations that range different nations might be impacted by line debates, prompting issues with site the board and assurance.

Social and Social Difficulties

14. **Disregard and Relinquishment:** Some social World Legacy Destinations experience the ill effects of disregard and surrender because of an absence of assets or political will to appropriately keep up with them.

15. **Evolving Customs:** Changes in neighborhood customs and lifestyles can affect social legacy. Modernization might prompt the relinquishment of conventional practices and designs.

16. **Social and Strict Contentions:** Social and strict struggles can prompt the deliberate annihilation of social legacy, as seen in different verifiable occasions.

Preservation Difficulties

17. **Asset Requirements:** Numerous nations miss the mark on assets and ability to actually oversee and safeguard their Reality Legacy Destinations. This can bring about deficient preservation endeavors.

18. **Adjusting Protection and Improvement:** Finding some kind of harmony between preserving World Legacy Destinations and meeting the monetary necessities of nearby networks can be testing, especially in agricultural nations.

19. **Documentation and Exploration:** Progressing research is fundamental for the protection of social and normal legacy. Insufficient documentation and research can block viable protection endeavors.
    Lawful and Administrative Difficulties

20. **Absence of Lawful Security:** now and again, World Legacy Destinations might areas of strength for need insurances or implementation systems, conveying them powerless against intimidations.

21. **Inadequate Guidelines:** In any event, when lawful securities exist, administrative structures might be insufficient or inadequately authorized, considering exercises that hurt the site.
    The travel industry and Guest The executives

22. **Absence of Maintainable The travel industry:** Numerous World Legacy Locales battle with adjusting the advantages of the travel industry with the requirement for site protection. Impractical the travel industry practices can harm both regular and social legacy.

23. **Absence of Guest Instruction:** Deficient guest training and mindfulness about the significance of saving World Legacy Locales can prompt unexpected harm.
    Lacking Administration and Arranging

24. **Insufficient Administration Plans:** Some World Legacy Destinations might need thorough administration plans, conveying it trying to address intimidations and carry out protection gauges really.

25. **Absence of Neighborhood Commitment:** Compelling site the board frequently requires commitment with nearby networks. The shortfall of local area association can upset protection endeavors.

Examples of overcoming adversity and Protection Endeavors

Notwithstanding these difficulties and dangers, there are various examples of overcoming adversity that feature the adequacy of preservation endeavors. These victories show that with commitment, global participation, and economical practices, World Legacy Destinations can be saved for people in the future to appreciate and appreciate.

The recuperation of the dark wolf populace in Yellowstone Public Park in the US after effective renewed introduction endeavors.

The reclamation of Venice's memorable structures through projects like the "MoSE" framework, which shields the city from flooding.

The security and preservation of the Virunga Public Park in the Vote based Republic of Congo, home to jeopardized mountain gorillas.

The cooperative endeavors to preserve the memorable city of Timbuktu in Mali, protecting its social fortunes from struggle related harm.

5.1 Examination of common threats to World Heritage Sites:

Assessment of Normal Dangers to World Legacy Destinations

World Legacy Destinations, perceived for their exceptional widespread worth, are not safe to a heap of dangers that risk their protection and honesty. These dangers originate from different sources, including normal cycles, human exercises, and international elements. In this far reaching assessment, we will dive into the most widely recognized dangers that World Legacy Destinations face and investigate their suggestions for these loved spots.

Environmental Change

Environmental change presents one of the most critical and extensive dangers to World Legacy Destinations. Its effects are complex and include:

Climbing Temperatures: Expanding worldwide temperatures can adjust biological systems and jeopardize species that are adjusted to explicit climatic circumstances.

Ocean Level Ascent: Beach front World Legacy Destinations are especially helpless against ocean level ascent, which can bring about disintegration, flooding, and the deficiency of social legacy.

Outrageous Climate Occasions: More regular and serious climate occasions, like tropical storms, floods, and rapidly spreading fires, can make quick and disastrous harm both normal and social destinations.

Coral Dying: Coral reefs, imperative parts of marine environments, are defenseless to coral fading because of increasing ocean temperatures, prompting the deficiency of biodiversity.

Ice sheet Retreat: Glacial masses, which hold social and hydrological importance, are withdrawing overall because of climbing temperatures, influencing the scenes of rocky World Legacy Locales.

Cataclysmic events

Cataclysmic events, both unexpected and capricious, represent a quick danger to World Legacy Destinations:

Seismic tremors: Quakes can make primary harm memorable structures and social landmarks, as found in the annihilation of Kathmandu's Durbar Square in Nepal in 2015.

Volcanic Emissions: Volcanic ejections can cover social and normal destinations under debris and magma, modifying their scenes and environments.

Tidal waves: Seaside World Legacy Locales are helpless to waves, which can bring about destroying flooding and harm to social legacy.

Typhoons and Tropical storms: Cyclonic tempests can make broad harm both normal and social destinations in their way, as exemplified by Typhoon Katrina in the US.

Fierce blazes: Rapidly spreading fires can compromise both normal and social legacy, obliterating authentic designs, antiquities, and environments.

Human-Actuated Dangers

Human-actuated dangers emerge from different exercises and improvements:

Over-The travel industry: The flood in worldwide the travel industry has prompted over-the travel industry at numerous World Legacy Destinations. Congestion can bring about ecological debasement, harm to social legacy, and stress on nearby assets.

Improvement Tension: Urbanization, foundation projects, and unregulated advancement can infringe upon World Legacy Locales, adjusting their scenes and undermining their legitimacy.

Contamination: Contamination from ventures, farming, and metropolitan regions can hurt both regular and social legacy. Air and water contamination can consume noteworthy designs and mischief environments.

Deforestation: Deforestation and living space misfortune can fundamentally affect regular World Legacy Destinations, prompting territory misfortune, species annihilation, and disturbed environments.

Criminal operations: Poaching, unlawful logging, and plundering of social antiques present critical dangers. These exercises can exhaust biodiversity and deny the universe of social fortunes.

International Difficulties

International difficulties come from political struggles and questions:

Furnished Struggle: World Legacy Locales situated in areas of equipped clash face quick and serious dangers. They can be harmed or obliterated purposefully as a feature of military activities.

Common Distress: Common agitation and political shakiness can disturb the administration and security of World Legacy Locales, making them powerless against plundering and harm.

Line Debates: Transnational World Legacy Locales that range numerous nations might be impacted by line questions, prompting issues with site the board and insurance.

Social and Social Difficulties

Social and social difficulties emerge from changing practices and clashes:

Disregard and Deserting: Some social World Legacy Destinations experience the ill effects of disregard and surrender because of an absence of assets or political will to appropriately keep up with them.

Evolving Customs: Changes in neighborhood customs and lifestyles can affect social legacy. Modernization might prompt the surrender of customary practices and designs.

Social and Strict Contentions: Social and strict struggles can prompt the deliberate obliteration of social legacy, as seen in different verifiable examples.

Protection Difficulties

Protection challenges are connected with the insurance and conservation of World Legacy Locales:

Asset Limitations: Many site the board specialists work with restricted assets, making it trying to execute far reaching protection and the executives designs successfully.

Adjusting Protection and Improvement: Finding some kind of harmony between financial turn of events and site safeguarding is much of the time testing, especially in non-industrial nations.

Documentation and Exploration: Continuous examination is fundamental for the protection of social and regular legacy. Deficient documentation and research can obstruct viable protection endeavors.

Lawful and Administrative Difficulties

Lawful and administrative difficulties relate to the deficiency of existing legitimate insurances and guidelines:

Absence of Lawful Assurance: at times, World Legacy Destinations might serious areas of strength for need securities or implementation components, conveying them defenseless against intimidations.

Insufficient Guidelines: In any event, when legitimate securities exist, administrative structures might be incapable or ineffectively upheld, considering exercises that hurt the site.

The travel industry and Guest The board

The travel industry and guest the executives challenges are related with dealing with the inundation of sightseers:

Absence of Practical The travel industry: Numerous World Legacy Destinations battle with adjusting the advantages of the travel industry with the requirement for site safeguarding. Unreasonable the travel industry practices can harm both regular and social legacy.

Absence of Guest Instruction: Inadequate guest training and mindfulness about the significance of saving World Legacy Locales can prompt accidental harm.

Lacking Administration and Arranging

Insufficient administration and arranging difficulties include issues with site the executives:

Deficient Administration Plans: Some World Legacy Destinations might need far reaching the executives plans, conveying it trying to address intimidations and carry out protection gauges really.

Absence of Nearby Commitment: Successful site the board frequently requires commitment with neighborhood networks. The shortfall of local area inclusion can obstruct protection endeavors.

Examples of overcoming adversity and Preservation Endeavors

In spite of these difficulties and dangers, there are various examples of overcoming adversity that feature the viability of protection endeavors. These victories exhibit that with commitment, global collaboration, and supportable practices, World Legacy Destinations can be safeguarded for people in the future to appreciate and appreciate.

The recuperation of the dark wolf populace in Yellowstone Public Park in the US after effective renewed introduction endeavors.

The rebuilding of Venice's noteworthy structures through projects like the "MoSE" framework, which safeguards the city from flooding.

The assurance and protection of the Virunga Public Park in the Popularity based Republic of Congo, home to imperiled mountain gorillas.

The cooperative endeavors to monitor the noteworthy city of Timbuktu in Mali, protecting its social fortunes from struggle related harm.

5.2 Climate change.

Environmental Change: A Worldwide Test to World Legacy Destinations

Environmental change is one of the most squeezing and broad difficulties confronting our planet today. Its significant effect reaches out to World Legacy Locales, spots of extraordinary social, normal, or blended esteem perceived for their importance to humankind. These destinations are progressively power-less against the results of an evolving environment, with suggestions for both their natural honesty and social legacy. In this assessment, we will dive into the impacts of environmental influence on World Legacy Destinations and in-vestigate the systems being utilized to moderate these dangers.

The Environmental Change Challenge

1. **Increasing Temperatures**

   Increasing worldwide temperatures are a sign of environmental change. As temperatures increment, numerous World Legacy Locales face a scope of difficulties:

   Environmental Movements: Climbing temperatures can upset biological systems and modify species dispersions, jeopardizing exceptional verdure found inside World Legacy Locales.

   Softening Glacial masses: Sloping locales with ice sheets, like the Swiss Alps, are seeing sped up glacial mass liquefy, prompting changes in water accessibility and scene change.

   Social Effect: The effects reach out to social destinations, where ex-panded temperatures can speed up the weakening of notable designs and works of art.

2. **Ocean Level Ascent**

   Waterfront World Legacy Locales are especially vulnerable to the ocean level ascent, an immediate outcome of an unnatural weather change:

Disintegration and Flooding: Higher ocean levels lead to waterfront disintegration and expanded flooding, compromising beach front social locales like Venice, Italy, and normal destinations like the Wadden Ocean.
Saline Interruption: Rising ocean levels can likewise bring about salt-water interruption into freshwater environments, disturbing fragile biological equilibriums.

3. **Outrageous Climate Occasions**
Environmental change is connected to the expanded recurrence and power of outrageous climate occasions:
Typhoons and Hurricanes: Seaside World Legacy Destinations are in danger from additional strong tornadoes, for example, the Incomparable Boundary Reef in Australia, which is undermined by additional continuous and serious tempests.
Out of control fires: Drier circumstances and delayed heatwaves add to fierce blazes, imperiling normal locales like the Redwood Public and State Parks in California, USA.

4. **Coral Blanching**

Hotter sea temperatures have prompted coral fading occasions, which have extreme ramifications for marine World Legacy Locales:
Extraordinary Boundary Reef: One of the most notable regular World Legacy Destinations, the Incomparable Obstruction Reef, faces far reaching coral blanching, imperiling its biodiversity and environment wellbeing.

The Ramifications for World Legacy Locales
The effect of environmental influence on World Legacy Destinations is complex, with both natural and social results:

1. **Biological Effect**
Biodiversity Misfortune: Environmental change disturbs biological systems, imperiling the assorted widely varied vegetation found inside World Legacy Locales. Species that can't adjust or move might confront termination.
Territory Obliteration: Increasing temperatures, ocean level ascent, and changing atmospheric conditions can prompt living space annihilation, affecting the honesty of normal destinations like the Galápagos Islands.
Disturbed Biological system Administrations: Environments inside World Legacy Destinations offer fundamental types of assistance, like water purging and fertilization. Environmental change can upset these administrations, influencing neighborhood networks and biodiversity.

2. **Social Effect**

Underlying Disintegration: Noteworthy designs and social ancient rarities are defenseless to the actual effects of environmental change, including temperature limits, moistness, and ocean level ascent.

Social Interruption: Environmental change can disturb social practices and customs attached to World Legacy Destinations, influencing the social character of nearby networks.

Loss of Legitimacy: Social destinations might lose their genuineness as rising ocean levels or disintegration force the movement or remaking of memorable designs.

Methodologies for Moderation and Transformation

Perceiving the pressing need to address environmental change, endeavors are in progress to moderate its effect on World Legacy Locales:

1. **Environment Versatile Preparation**

   Variation Plans: Site the executives specialists are creating transformation intends to shield World Legacy Destinations. These plans incorporate measures to safeguard against disintegration, moderate flood dangers, and ration water assets.

   Reasonable Turn of events: Manageable advancement rehearses expect to offset financial development with the protection of normal and social legacy, diminishing the effect of human exercises on the environment.

2. **Preservation and Rebuilding**

   Biological system Rebuilding: Protection endeavors center around reestablishing environments and natural surroundings inside World Legacy Destinations to help biodiversity and adjust to evolving conditions.

   Underlying Preservation: Social locales go through rebuilding and protection endeavors to guarantee their primary respectability and shield social legacy.

3. **Supportable The travel industry**

   Guest The executives: Economical the travel industry rehearses look to restrict the quantity of guests to World Legacy Destinations, forestalling over-the travel industry and related ecological debasement.

   Guest Instruction: Bringing issues to light among guests about the effect of environmental influence on World Legacy Locales supports capable way of behaving and conservation endeavors.

4. **Worldwide Cooperation**

   Sharing Accepted procedures: UNESCO energizes the dividing of best practices between nations and site the executives specialists to address environmental change altogether.

   Logical Exploration: Continuous logical examination is fundamental for understanding the particular dangers presented by environmental change to individual World Legacy Destinations and creating custom fitted arrangements.

5. **Local area Commitment**

Nearby Information: Connecting with neighborhood networks and coordinating conventional information into protection and variation systems upgrades the versatility of World Legacy Locales.

Local area Based Protection: Engaging nearby networks to play a functioning job in site conservation encourages a feeling of pride and shared liability.

Examples of overcoming adversity

Regardless of the critical difficulties presented by environmental change, there are occasions where relief and variation endeavors have borne natural product:

Chitwan Public Park, Nepal: Protection endeavors in this World Legacy Site have safeguarded imperiled species and their environments while connecting with nearby networks in conservation.

Mont-Holy person Michel and its Inlet, France: Inventive designing arrangements have been utilized to resolve the issue of sedimentation and work on the site's flexibility to rising ocean levels.

Everglades Public Park, USA: Environment reclamation projects in the Everglades have further developed water stream, helping biodiversity and water quality.

5.3 Tourism pressures.

The travel industry Tensions on World Legacy Destinations: Adjusting Safeguarding and Appearance

The travel industry is a situation with two sides for World Legacy Locales. On one hand, it brings monetary advantages, advances social trade, and raises worldwide mindfulness. Then again, uncontrolled the travel industry can prompt congestion, ecological debasement, and harm to social legacy. Finding some kind of harmony between bridling the upsides of the travel industry while protecting the respectability of these loved destinations is a test looked by site the executives specialists, legislatures, and the worldwide local area. In this investigation, we will dive into the tensions that travel industry applies on World Legacy Destinations and the systems utilized to oversee and moderate these effects.

The Advantages of The travel industry

The travel industry can carry a huge number of advantages to World Legacy Destinations:

Monetary Development: The travel industry produces income, making position and supporting neighborhood organizations. This monetary lift can assist with financing preservation endeavors and work on the vocations of nearby networks.

Social Trade: Travelers from around the world give open doors to social trade. They find out about the legacy and customs of the host local area, encouraging comprehension and enthusiasm for assorted societies.

Worldwide Mindfulness: The travel industry advances worldwide attention to World Legacy Destinations. Worldwide guests frequently share their encounters, raising the profile of these destinations and possibly drawing in help and subsidizing for their conservation.

The Difficulties of The travel industry

Regardless of the advantages, the travel industry presents a few difficulties for World Legacy Destinations:

Packing: Well known destinations can become stuffed, prompting a reduced guest experience and ecological corruption. For instance, the noteworthy focus of Rome, a World Legacy Site, faces serious congestion.

Ecological Effect: Expanded people walking through can hurt delicate biological systems and normal living spaces, as seen in Machu Picchu, Peru, where unregulated the travel industry impacted the site's environment.

Social Disintegration: Extreme the travel industry can dissolve the validness and social customs of nearby networks. The strain to take special care of sightseers might prompt the commercialization of social practices.

Foundation Advancement: The interest for the travel industry framework, like lodgings and transportation, can bring about rambling improvements that adjust the person and scene of World Legacy Destinations.

Mileage: High appearance rates negatively affect noteworthy designs and antiquities, prompting actual crumbling. The Pyramids of Giza, Egypt, have experienced the effect of travelers throughout the long term.

Reasonable The travel industry Practices

To address these difficulties and guarantee the supportability of the travel industry in World Legacy Locales, different procedures and practices are utilized:

Guest The executives: Carrying out guest shares or planned passage frameworks helps control the quantity of guests, forestalling packing.

Foundation Advancement: Supportable framework arranging centers around limiting the natural effect of improvement while giving fundamental conveniences to guests.

Training and Understanding: Guest instruction programs bring issues to light about mindful the travel industry and the meaning of the site, empowering aware way of behaving.

Nearby Commitment: Connecting with neighborhood networks in the travel industry arranging and the board guarantees that monetary advantages are shared and social practices are protected.

Protection Charges: Extra charges and income sharing systems can produce assets for site preservation and backing neighborhood networks.

Examples of overcoming adversity in Economical The travel industry

A few World Legacy Destinations have effectively executed manageable the travel industry rehearses:

Galápagos Islands, Ecuador: Severe guest amounts, directed visits, and eco-accommodating practices have safeguarded this extraordinary regular site.

Bhutan: The country's travel industry strategy centers around high-esteem, low-influence the travel industry, guaranteeing that guests regard social and ecological responsive qualities.

Blenheim Castle, Joined Realm: This social site urges guests to investigate the bequest's regular scenes and nurseries, giving an illustration of agreeable incorporation among legacy and the travel industry.

5.4 Armed conflict and vandalism.

Outfitted Struggle and Defacement: Dangers to World Legacy Locales

World Legacy Destinations, celebrated for their social and normal importance to humankind, are not insusceptible to the disastrous powers of outfitted struggle and defacement. These dangers can have disastrous outcomes, prompting hopeless harm to indispensable legacy. In this assessment, we will dig into the difficulties presented by furnished struggle and defacing to World Legacy Locales, the effect on these fortunes, and the endeavors to safeguard and save them.

Outfitted Struggle: A Critical Danger

1. **Purposeful Obliteration**

   Outfitted struggle frequently brings about the purposeful obliteration of social legacy, driven by different inspirations:

   Emblematic Objective: Social legacy is focused on as an emblematic portrayal of a local area's personality, history, or religion, making it an ideal objective for warriors looking to disintegrate the confidence and social character of their rivals.

   Monetary Increase: Plundering of social relics can furnish soldiers with a type of revenue through the unlawful artifacts exchange.

2. **Blow-back**

   In any event, when not purposely designated, World Legacy Destinations are in danger of experiencing blow-back during outfitted clashes:

   Unstable Harm: Blasts from weapons can make primary harm notable structures and landmarks, like the annihilation of Aleppo's noteworthy bastion during the Syrian Nationwide conflict.

   Ecological Effect: Fighting can prompt natural debasement, affecting normal destinations like Virunga Public Park in the Popularity based Republic of Congo, home to jeopardized mountain gorillas.

3. **Struggle Incited Dislodging**

Outfitted struggle can prompt the relocation of neighborhood networks living close to World Legacy Destinations, bringing about the disregard and surrender of these locales.
Defacement: A Danger from The inside

1. **Spray painting and Destruction**
   Destructive incidents, including spray painting and ruination, can pollute the social and verifiable meaning of World Legacy Destinations:
   Spray painting: Hoodlums might shower paint or cut spray painting onto noteworthy structures and designs, lessening their tasteful and authentic worth.
   Ruination: Demonstrations of mutilation, for example, working on figures or engravings, can hurt extremely durable social legacy.
2. **Robbery and Plundering**

Defacement additionally incorporates burglary and plundering of social curios:
Craftsmanship Burglary: Important works of art and ancient rarities are taken from exhibition halls and social locales, frequently vanishing into the bootleg market.
Archeological Plundering: Illegal digging and plundering of archeological destinations can bring about the deficiency of important authentic and social data.
Influences on World Legacy Destinations
The effect of equipped clash and defacement on World Legacy Locales is significant and boundless:

1. **Irreversible Misfortune**
   The obliteration and defacement of social and normal legacy bring about irreversible misfortune, deleting the exceptional history and meaning of these locales.
2. **Interruption of Social Congruity**
   Social legacy addresses the progression of mankind's set of experiences. Its obliteration disturbs the social progression of nearby networks and the world overall.
3. **Financial Results**
   The deficiency of World Legacy Destinations because of equipped clash and defacing has financial outcomes, including decreased the travel industry income and expected lost pay from social and authentic conservation.

4. Natural Corruption
Equipped struggle can prompt ecological corruption, influencing regular World Legacy Destinations and the biodiversity they harbor.

5. Social Character

The purposeful obliteration of social legacy disintegrates the social personality of networks, influencing their feeling of having a place and association with the past.

Insurance and Conservation Endeavors
Endeavors to safeguard and protect World Legacy Destinations from equipped struggle and defacing include:

1. Global Shows
Peaceful accords, like the 1954 Hague Show for the Assurance of Social Property In case of Equipped Clash and its conventions, give lawful systems to the security of social legacy during furnished struggle.

2. Site The executives Plans
Viable site the board plans incorporate gamble evaluations and methodologies to defend legacy during clashes. These plans might incorporate clearing of important antiques and support of weak designs.

3. Worldwide Mindfulness
Raising worldwide mindfulness about the outcomes of outfitted struggle and defacing is essential. Global associations, states, and common society assume key parts in supporting for legacy assurance.

4. Post-Struggle Restoration
After clashes, recovery endeavors include the reclamation and remaking of harmed legacy destinations, for example, the rebuilding of social milestones in post-war Europe.

5. Local area Commitment

Connecting with nearby networks in legacy security cultivates a feeling of pride and shared liability regarding protecting these destinations.

Examples of overcoming adversity
In spite of the difficulties, there have been remarkable triumphs in safeguarding World Legacy Destinations:

The Bamiyan Buddhas, Afghanistan: In the wake of being deliberately annihilated by the Taliban, endeavors are in progress to recreate the notorious Buddha sculptures.

The Old City of Dubrovnik, Croatia: Following broad harm during the Balkan clashes, the city has been meticulously reestablished, protecting its social legacy.

5.5 Case studies illustrating these challenges.

Contextual analyses Representing Difficulties to World Legacy Destinations

A few contextual investigations feature the difficulties presented by outfitted struggle and defacing to World Legacy Destinations, revealing insight into the staggering effect of these dangers and the endeavors to safeguard and protect these esteemed spots.

1. **Palmyra, Syria**
   Furnished Struggle and Deliberate Annihilation
   The old city of Palmyra, an UNESCO World Legacy Site in Syria, was once a flourishing focal point of exchange and culture. Nonetheless, it turned into a grievous image of the obliteration brought about by furnished struggle and purposeful defacing. During the Syrian Nationwide conflict, the radical gathering ISIS assumed command over Palmyra in 2015.
   They purposely focused on and obliterated various memorable designs, including the notorious Sanctuary of Bel and the Curve of Win, which had represented hundreds of years. These destructive incidents were planned to delete social variety and legacy, as well as to produce income through the illegal offer of relics.
   Endeavors to Protect and Reestablish:
   Global judgment and public objection prodded endeavors to archive the harm and save what survived from Palmyra's legacy.
   After the freedom of Palmyra from ISIS control, the Syrian government, with global help, started reclamation and remaking undertakings to modify the harmed structures and safeguard the leftover ancient rarities.
   The instance of Palmyra highlights the significance of worldwide collaboration and obligation to saving legacy, even despite furnished struggle and deliberate obliteration.

2. **Bagan, Myanmar**
   Defacing and Social Legacy Conservation
   Bagan, an old city in Myanmar, is eminent for its tremendous archeological site highlighting large number of Buddhist sanctuaries and pagodas. Notwithstanding, as of late, Bagan confronted an alternate test: defacing from sightseers. Occurrences of sightseers getting on and mutilating the noteworthy designs with spray painting turned into a worry, compromising the trustworthiness of this UNESCO World Legacy Site.
   Endeavors to Save and Instruct:
   Nearby specialists executed stricter guidelines and expanded fines for vandalizing memorable destinations.
   Guest training programs were acquainted with bring issues to light about capable the travel industry and the significance of protecting social

legacy.

While Bagan confronted defacement from sightseers instead of equipped clash, this case highlights the significance of proactive measures to safeguard World Legacy Destinations from different dangers, including those originating from guest conduct.

3. **Timbuktu, Mali**

Outfitted Struggle and Social Conservation

Timbuktu, a memorable city in Mali, is known for its old libraries and compositional fortunes. Notwithstanding, during the outfitted clash in Mali in 2012, radical gatherings involved the city and deliberately harmed social legacy locales. The extremely old original copies put away in Timbuktu's libraries confronted the danger of annihilation, as did strict and social landmarks.

Endeavors to Save and Modify:

Worldwide associations, states, and neighborhood networks cooperated to protect the original copies, with many being pirated to somewhere safe and secure.

After the city was freed from fanatic control, reclamation endeavors started to modify harmed designs and safeguard Timbuktu's social legacy.

The instance of Timbuktu exhibits the versatility of networks and the significance of worldwide help in securing and reestablishing social legacy in the consequence of outfitted struggle.

These contextual analyses feature the different and complex difficulties that World Legacy Locales face, going from purposeful obliteration during equipped struggles to defacing by vacationers. Notwithstanding, they likewise underscore the versatility of these destinations and the decided endeavors to safeguard and protect our common social and normal legacy. These difficulties highlight the significance of proceeded with worldwide collaboration, mindfulness, and obligation to defending these uncommon spots for people in the future.

CHAPTER 6

Preservation Success Stories

Conservation Examples of overcoming adversity: Protecting Our Reality Legacy

In the midst of the bunch difficulties that compromise the uprightness of World Legacy Locales, there are rousing examples of overcoming adversity that show mankind's ability to save and safeguard these remarkable spots. These accounts act as encouraging signs, showing that with commitment, resourcefulness, and global collaboration, protecting our social and normal legacy for people in the future is conceivable. In this investigation, we will dig into a few striking protection examples of overcoming adversity from around the world.

1. **Venice and the MOSE Undertaking, Italy**

   The Test: Venice, a city of unmatched magnificence and social importance, has long wrestled with the dangers of rising ocean levels and flooding. The steady immersion of the memorable city represented a critical gamble to its building treasures and social legacy.

   The Arrangement: because of this test, Italy left on the aggressive MOSE (Modulo Sperimentale Elettromeccanico) project. MOSE comprises of a progression of retractable hindrances introduced at the doors to the Venetian Tidal pond. These hindrances can be raised during elevated tides to hinder the inflow of seawater, shielding the city from flooding.

   The Achievement: The MOSE project addresses a surprising designing accomplishment that expects to moderate the quick danger of flooding in Venice. While the venture has confronted postponements and discussions, it shows the obligation to protecting this notable World Legacy Site. It likewise fills in as an image of how creative arrangements can be utilized to shield social legacy from natural difficulties.

2. **Yellowstone Public Park, USA**

   The Test: Yellowstone Public Park, the world's most memorable public park and an UNESCO World Legacy Site, confronted an overwhelming test in the late twentieth 100 years — the expected termination of the dark wolf. By the mid-twentieth hundred years, dark wolves had been deliberately annihilated from the recreation area, disturbing the recreation area's environment.

The Arrangement: In 1995 and 1996, a noteworthy exertion was sent off to once again introduce dim wolves into Yellowstone. This renewed introduction expected to reestablish the biological equilibrium by controlling the number of inhabitants in elk, which had flooded in the wolves' nonattendance. The task included catching and migrating wolves from Canada to Yellowstone.

The Achievement: The renewed introduction of dim wolves significantly affects Yellowstone's environment. It prompted a "trophic outpouring," where the presence of wolves changed the way of behaving of elk, which thus impacted vegetation and other untamed life. The rebuilding of this dominant hunter kept a better and more different biological system in the recreation area. The outcome of the Yellowstone wolf renewed introduction has turned into a worldwide preservation model, showing the basic job of cornerstone species in safeguarding regular legacy.

3. **Petra, Jordan**
The Test: Petra, the old city cut into rose-red precipices of southern Jordan, is an archeological marvel and an UNESCO World Legacy Site. Be that as it may, the site confronted the test of disintegration and primary flimsiness because of its extraordinary geographical setting and enduring cycles.

The Arrangement: Petra went through a broad preservation exertion that elaborate a mix of logical exploration, adjustment measures, and the utilization of conventional structure strategies. Specialists, archeologists, and traditionalists cooperated to distinguish weak designs and execute measures to guarantee their soundness.

The Achievement: Petra's protection endeavors have been exceptionally effective. Inventive procedures, for example, the utilization of PC displaying to survey underlying trustworthiness, have been utilized close by customary techniques like lime mortar to fix harmed veneers. The site's social legacy stays in salvageable shape, permitting guests to investigate this old marvel. The instance of Petra grandstands the significance of a multidisciplinary way to deal with legacy conservation, mixing present day innovation with conventional craftsmanship.

4. **Extraordinary Boundary Reef, Australia**
The Test: The Incomparable Hindrance Reef, the world's biggest coral reef framework and an UNESCO World Legacy Site, confronted desperate dangers from coral dying, overfishing, and contamination. Climbing ocean

temperatures because of environmental change put the reef's sensitive biological system in danger.

The Arrangement: Australia has executed a scope of preservation measures to safeguard the Incomparable Hindrance Reef. These incorporate severe fishing guidelines, marine safeguarded regions, water quality improvement drives, and endeavors to diminish fossil fuel byproducts.

The Achievement: The preservation endeavors have yielded positive outcomes. While the reef actually faces continuous difficulties, for example, coral fading occasions, the execution of defensive measures has settled and recuperate a portion of the harmed coral regions. The Incomparable Boundary Reef's story exhibits the significance of proactive preservation estimates even with environmental change and underlines the requirement for worldwide activity to alleviate the effects of increasing ocean temperatures.

5. **Angkor Wat, Cambodia**

The Test: Angkor Wat, an engineering wonder and UNESCO World Legacy Site in Cambodia, confronted critical difficulties, including infringement by vegetation and the disintegration of its unpredictable sandstone carvings due to enduring.

The Arrangement: Preservation endeavors at Angkor Wat have involved the getting free from infringing vegetation and the utilization of imaginative procedures, like utilizing an extraordinary biodegradable paper to safeguard fragile carvings during reclamation.

The Achievement: The reclamation of Angkor Wat has been profoundly effective, guaranteeing the site's proceeded with primary respectability and saving its perplexing carvings. The instance of Angkor Wat grandstands the significance of progressing support and preservation endeavors to shield social legacy destinations.

6.1 Inspiring stories of successful preservation and restoration efforts: Motivating Accounts of Fruitful Conservation and Rebuilding Endeavors

All through the world, there are astounding accounts of fruitful conservation and rebuilding endeavors that have saved and revived valuable social and normal legacy.

These undertakings stand as demonstrations of human inventiveness, assurance, and a profound obligation to defending our past and the climate for people in the future. In this investigation, we will dive into five moving stories that feature the victories of safeguarding and rebuilding.

1. **The Reclamation of the Sistine House of prayer, Vatican City**

The Test: The Sistine Church, situated inside Vatican City, houses probably the most notorious frescoes on the planet, painted by the incomparable Renaissance craftsman Michelangelo. Over hundreds of years, these show-stoppers had experienced the gathering of residue, soil, and light ash. The varieties had dulled, and the frescoes were in danger of additional weakening.

The Arrangement: In 1980, an enormous rebuilding project was started under the direction of the Vatican Exhibition halls. A group of specialists set out on the meticulous undertaking of cleaning and reestablishing Michelangelo's frescoes utilizing progressed methods and fastidious consideration. The rebuilding system included the utilization of exceptionally evolved solvents and magnifying instruments to eliminate layers of grime without hurting the first fine art.

The Achievement: The reclamation of the Sistine Sanctuary was a staggering achievement. The venture revealed the brightness of Michelangelo's work, reestablishing the clear tones and multifaceted subtleties to their unique greatness. The Sistine House of prayer presently remains as a reference point of workmanship protection and a demonstration of the persevering through force of human inventiveness.

2. **The Resurrection of Machu Picchu, Peru**

The Test: Machu Picchu, the notable Incan stronghold settled in the Andes Mountains, confronted various dangers throughout the long term, including primary unsteadiness, disintegration, and the effects of the travel industry.

The Arrangement: The Peruvian government, as a team with worldwide associations and specialists, sent off an exhaustive conservation and rebuilding exertion. The undertaking included fastidious stone-by-stone evaluation and remaking of harmed structures, as well as feasible the travel industry the executives.

The Achievement: Machu Picchu has been restored and protected for people in the future. It has turned into a model for mindful the travel industry, restricting the quantity of guests and guaranteeing that the site's interesting environment and social legacy are safeguarded. The effective resurrection of Machu Picchu highlights the significance of proactive preservation measures and maintainable the travel industry rehearses.

3. **The Recuperation of the Palais Garnier, France**

The Test: The Palais Garnier, a rich drama house in Paris, had experienced many years of disregard and deficient support. The structure's façade was defaced by contamination, while the inside had crumbled because of water harm, rot, and obsolete framework.

The Arrangement: A fastidious and broad rebuilding project was sent off in the late twentieth 100 years to take the Palais Garnier back to its previous greatness. Gifted craftsmans and skilled workers were utilized to fix and reproduce complicated embellishing components, while present day frameworks and innovation were coordinated into the structure's foundation.

Yet again the Achievement: The reclamation of the Palais Garnier has changed the show house into a lively social place. The venture resuscitated the structure's compositional magnificence as well as guaranteed that it stays a fundamental center for the performing expressions. It fills in as a demonstration of the significance of saving notable tourist spots and social establishments.

4. **The Renaissance of the Rwenzori Mountains, Uganda**

   The Test: The Rwenzori Mountains, otherwise called the "Mountains of the Moon," in Uganda had been affected by deforestation, environment debasement, and unlawful logging. The sensitive environment of these mountains, including interesting plant and creature species, was under danger.

   The Arrangement: Preservation associations, alongside nearby networks, started reforestation endeavors and reasonable land the executives rehearses. These endeavors intended to battle deforestation, safeguard biodiversity, and work on the vocations of the nearby populace.

   The Achievement: The Rwenzori Mountains have encountered an exceptional resurgence. Reforestation endeavors have restored the timberlands, giving territory to imperiled species, for example, the Rwenzori duiker and safeguarding the remarkable greenery of the district. The reclamation of this regular marvel shows the force of local area association and economical preservation rehearses.

5. **The Restoration of the Chesapeake Straight, USA**

The Test: The Chesapeake Straight, the biggest estuary in the US, confronted serious contamination, environment misfortune, and declining water quality because of urbanization, horticulture, and modern exercises.

The Arrangement: More than a very long while, an exhaustive reclamation exertion was sent off to address the difficulties confronting the Chesapeake Sound. This included decreasing supplement spillover, reestablishing wetlands and shellfish populaces, and executing severe natural guidelines.

The Achievement: The Chesapeake Sound's wellbeing has improved altogether. Water quality has expanded, shellfish populaces have bounced back, and endeavors to safeguard wetlands have helped various species. The rebuilding of this indispensable estuary fills in as a demonstration of the potential for natural recuperation through supported preservation endeavors.

6.2 The restoration of Venice and its lagoon, Italy.

The Rebuilding of Venice and Its Tidal pond: A Victory of Legacy Safeguarding

The city of Venice, prestigious for its stunning engineering, rich history, and many-sided organization of trenches, remains as quite possibly of the most notable and dearest social fortune on the planet. Be that as it may, Venice has confronted a novel and tireless test over now is the ideal time — the continuous danger of flooding and rising ocean levels. In this investigation, we will dig into the wonderful story of the reclamation of Venice and its tidal pond, a demonstration of human resourcefulness, global participation, and relentless commitment to safeguarding this UNESCO World Legacy Site.

The Test: Venice's Continuous Fight with Flooding

Venice, frequently alluded to as the "Drifting City," is based on an organization of 118 islands inside a tidal pond in the Adriatic Ocean. The city's notable structures, trenches, and spans have dazzled guests for a really long time. Be that as it may, the city's exceptional area likewise makes it profoundly powerless against the standard flooding brought about by a mix of variables:

Maturing Framework: Venice's mind boggling arrangement of waterways and tidal ponds depends on a maturing foundation, including wooden pilings that help structures. After some time, these pilings have disintegrated, making the city powerless to subsidence.

Acqua Alta: The "acqua alta" peculiarity happens when elevated tides and tempest floods make seawater flood the city. This is turning out to be more regular because of rising ocean levels brought about by environmental change.

The travel industry Strain: Venice's prominence as a vacationer location has prompted the congestion of specific regions, adding to soil compaction and subsidence.

Modern Exercises: The extraction of groundwater from wells on the Venetian central area has additionally added to land subsidence.

These difficulties compromised the city's structural fortunes, its social legacy, and the day to day routine of Venetians. The requirement for a far reaching and creative arrangement turned out to be progressively critical.

The MOSE Undertaking: An Intense Designing Wonder

In light of Venice's continuous fight with flooding, Italy left on an aggressive venture known as MOSE, or "Modulo Sperimentale Elettromeccanico" (Exploratory Electromechanical Module). The MOSE project meant to safeguard Venice and its tidal pond from the danger of elevated tides and flooding through the development of versatile hindrances at the passageways to the tidal pond.

The MOSE Boundary Framework:

The MOSE framework comprises of a progression of boundaries, intended to ascend from the seabed to obstruct the elevated tides when required. Key highlights of the MOSE boundary framework include:

Pivoted Obstructions: Every boundary comprises of enormous, pivoted boards that can be loaded up with water to become light and afterward raised to shape a hindrance against approaching tides.

Bay Boundaries: Hindrances are decisively positioned at the three fundamental passages to the Venice Tidal pond — the Lido Bay, Malamocco Gulf, and Chioggia Channel.

Control Framework: A modern control framework screens weather patterns, tides, and water levels. At the point when elevated tides are anticipated, the hindrances are actuated to impede the inflow of seawater.

Execution Difficulties:

The MOSE project, started in 1980, confronted various difficulties, including designing intricacies, ecological worries, and monetary obstacles. A portion of the key difficulties included:

Guaranteeing the boundaries were viable with Venice's fragile environment.

Tending to worries about the natural effect of boundary development and activity.

Beating monetary and strategic issues to finish the task.

The Achievement: Safeguarding Venice and Its Legacy

Following quite a while of arranging, designing, and development, the MOSE project accomplished a critical achievement in 2021 when the boundaries were effectively tried in genuine circumstances. This noticeable an essential move toward shielding Venice from the overwhelming impacts of elevated tides and flooding. The fruitful execution of the MOSE boundary framework has a few striking accomplishments and suggestions:

Prompt Security: The MOSE hindrances are intended to give quick assurance during elevated tide occasions, diminishing the gamble of flooding in the notable downtown area.

Protection of Social Legacy: By defending Venice from flooding, the MOSE project guarantees the safeguarding of the city's social and compositional legacy, including its notable structures, fine art, and one of a kind metropolitan texture.

Financial Advantages: The insurance of Venice's memorable locales has critical monetary ramifications, as the travel industry is an indispensable industry for the city and the more extensive Veneto district.

Natural Contemplations: The task likewise incorporates measures to relieve possible ecological effects, like observing water quality and supporting the nearby biological system.

Global Participation: The MOSE project addresses a cooperative exertion, with commitments from designers, researchers, and specialists from Italy and all over the planet. It exhibits the significance of worldwide collaboration in tending to worldwide difficulties.

Challenges and Progressing Concerns

While the effective testing of the MOSE boundaries addresses a critical accomplishment, difficulties and concerns remain:

Support: The MOSE framework requires continuous upkeep to guarantee its usefulness and dependability. Sufficient subsidizing and assets are fundamental for long haul maintainability.

Ecological Effect: Kept checking and alleviation measures are important to address expected natural effects and guarantee the soundness of the tidal pond environment.

Environmental Change: The MOSE project tends to the momentum danger of elevated tides and flooding, yet the more extensive test of rising ocean levels because of environmental change requires worldwide activity and transformation systems.

Monetary Suitability: The Coronavirus pandemic fundamentally impacted Venice's travel industry, influencing the city's economy and bringing up issues about the drawn out financial feasibility of the MOSE project.

6.3 The recovery of Angkor Wat, Cambodia.

The Recuperation of Angkor Wat, Cambodia: A Story of Reclamation and Strength

Angkor Wat, the rambling sanctuary complex settled in the core of Cambodia's wilderness, remains as a structural wonder and an image of the country's rich history and social legacy. Be that as it may, the narrative of Angkor Wat isn't only one of loftiness and greatness; it is likewise a story of decline, deserting, and, eventually, momentous recuperation through broad reclamation endeavors.

In this investigation, we will dive into the tale of the recuperation of Angkor Wat, a demonstration of human devotion, global joint effort, and the persevering through soul of protection.

The Verifiable and Social Meaning of Angkor Wat

Angkor Wat, worked in the twelfth hundred years during the Khmer Realm's pinnacle, is the biggest strict landmark on the planet. This UNESCO World Legacy Site grandstands mind boggling engineering, dazzling bas-reliefs, and a one of a kind mix of Hindu and Buddhist iconography. It remains as a portrayal of the Khmer progress' structural and creative ability.

In any case, throughout the long term, Angkor Wat confronted a progression of difficulties that undermined its trustworthiness and social importance:

Normal Powers: The sanctuary complex was step by step recovered by the encompassing wilderness because of the Khmer Domain's decay, causing underlying unsteadiness and harm.

Struggle and Disregard: The complex persevered through times of contention and disregard, including during the nationwide conflict in Cambodia in the twentieth hundred years, prompting further crumbling.

The travel industry Effect: The site's notoriety as a vacationer location presented difficulties connected with protection, stuffing, and the likely effect on the delicate designs.

The Job of the Apsara Authority

The recuperation of Angkor Wat and the more extensive Angkor Archeological Park was started and supervised by the Apsara Authority, a Cambodian legislative association entrusted with the administration and insurance of the recreation area. The power's endeavors have been instrumental in the protection and rebuilding of Angkor Wat and encompassing sanctuaries.

Reclamation Endeavors: A Multidisciplinary Approach

The reclamation of Angkor Wat and the sanctuaries inside the Angkor Archeological Park included a multidisciplinary approach that joined conventional craftsmanship with present day innovation. Key parts of the rebuilding endeavors included:

1. **Documentation and Exploration**

   Intensive documentation and examination were led to figure out the first development methods, materials, and design highlights of the sanctuaries. This elaborate the utilization of verifiable records, archeological investigations, and innovative apparatuses like 3D examining.

2. **Underlying Adjustment**

   A large number of the sanctuary structures were in a condition of cutting edge rot, with disintegrating walls and breaking down establishments. Gifted experts and conservators painstakingly evaluated the state of the sanctuaries and carried out primary adjustment measures to forestall further breakdown.

3. **Stone Protection**

   Angkor Wat's mind boggling bas-reliefs and stone carvings were carefully reestablished. Talented stone bricklayers and carvers used conventional strategies to fix harmed segments while protecting the first craftsmanship.

4. **Preventive Measures**

   To shield the sanctuaries from future crumbling, preventive measures were set up. These included better waste frameworks to oversee water spillover and control the water table to forestall underlying harm.

5. **Site The board and Guest Schooling**

The administration of guest access and conduct inside the sanctuary complex turned into a need. Guidelines were executed to limit actual harm to the designs, and instructive projects were acquainted with bring issues to light among sightseers about the significance of capable the travel industry.

Achievement and Progressing Difficulties

The rebuilding endeavors at Angkor Wat have yielded critical triumphs:

Primary Trustworthiness: Large numbers of the sanctuaries, including Angkor Wat itself, have been balanced out and reestablished to a condition that guarantees their drawn out underlying honesty.

Social Recovery: The restoration of Angkor Wat has revived a feeling of social pride among Cambodians, and the complicated assumes an imperative part in the nation's character and the travel industry.

Worldwide Legacy: Angkor Wat's rebuilding and conservation have had worldwide importance, exhibiting the global local area's obligation to shielding social legacy.

Nonetheless, difficulties and concerns persevere:

Natural Factors: The heat and humidity and the effect of downpour and mugginess keep on presenting difficulties to the safeguarding of the stone designs and bas-reliefs.

The travel industry Tension: The ubiquity of Angkor Wat as a vacationer location stays high, and overseeing guest numbers while guaranteeing a quality encounter and legacy security stays a sensitive equilibrium.

Subsidizing and Assets: Progressing support and reclamation endeavors require reliable financing and assets. Guaranteeing that these assets are accessible in the long haul is fundamental.

Worldwide Legacy: Angkor Wat's rebuilding and protection have had worldwide importance, showing the global local area's obligation to shielding social legacy.

Examples from Angkor Wat

The narrative of Angkor Wat's recuperation offers a few important illustrations in the field of legacy conservation:

Global Cooperation: The reclamation endeavors at Angkor Wat benefited significantly from worldwide coordinated effort and skill. The association of UNESCO and different nations in giving subsidizing, specialized help, and skill features the significance of worldwide collaboration in legacy safeguarding.

Multidisciplinary Approach: Consolidating conventional craftsmanship with present day innovation and exploration was fundamental for the progress of the reclamation endeavors. A complete, multidisciplinary approach is significant in handling complex legacy protection challenges.

Manageable The travel industry: Dealing with the effect of the travel industry on social legacy is a continuous concern. Dependable the travel industry practices, schooling, and guest the board assume urgent parts in protecting delicate locales like Angkor Wat.

Social Personality: Social legacy destinations are not just verifiable curios but rather vital pieces of a local area's social character. The rebuilding of

Angkor Wat has reaffirmed the meaning of this social fortune to Cambodia and its kin.

The recuperation of Angkor Wat is a wonderful demonstration of the force of human assurance and the significance of shielding our common social legacy. It fills in as a rousing illustration of what can be accomplished when devoted people, associations, and countries meet up to save the fortunes of our past for people in the future to respect and appreciate. Angkor Wat, with its getting through excellence and rich history, remains as an image of Cambodia's strength and the persevering through worth of our social legacy.

6.4 The revitalization of the Historic Center of Oaxaca, Mexico.

The Renewal of the Noteworthy Focus of Oaxaca, Mexico: A Social Renaissance

The Notable Focal point of Oaxaca, Mexico, is an energetic embroidery of history, culture, and custom.

Settled in the southern piece of the country, Oaxaca City is famous for its provincial design, antiquated remains, and rich native legacy. Nonetheless, in the same way as other notable metropolitan communities, Oaxaca confronted difficulties, including disregard, metropolitan rot, and the requirement for modernization. In this investigation, we will dive into the noteworthy story of the rejuvenation of the Memorable Focus of Oaxaca, a story of social renaissance, conservation, and local area driven change.

The Social Meaning of Oaxaca

The Noteworthy Focus of Oaxaca, assigned an UNESCO World Legacy Site in 1987, holds significant social and verifiable importance. It is a gold mine of engineering ponders, including very much safeguarded frontier structures with mind boggling veneers and rich patios. The city's Extravagant temples, for example, the Santo Domingo Church and the Basilica of Oaxaca, stand as compositional pearls, mirroring the combination of European and native styles.

Oaxaca's social legacy reaches out past its engineering. The city is a lively center for customary expressions and specialties, including multifaceted materials, stoneware, and flawless Oaxacan cooking, praised for its flavors and utilization of neighborhood fixings like mole sauce and mezcal.

The Difficulties of Metropolitan Rot

Notwithstanding its social extravagance, Oaxaca's Noteworthy Center confronted critical difficulties:

Metropolitan Rot: Throughout the long term, portions of the downtown area had fallen into deterioration. Notable structures experienced disregard, and framework, including streets and utilities, required modernization.

Blockage and Contamination: The city's restricted roads and restricted stopping offices prompted gridlock and contamination, lessening the personal satisfaction for occupants and reducing the guest experience.

Financial Incongruities: Oaxaca is home to a different populace, including native networks. Financial abberations and difficulties in safeguarding conventional jobs were issues that required consideration.

Safeguarding of Social Legacy: While Oaxaca's social legacy was a wellspring of pride, it likewise required insurance against the tensions of urbanization and modernization.

The Oaxaca Renaissance: Key Drives

The renewal of Oaxaca's Memorable Center is a demonstration of the responsibility of nearby specialists, local area associations, and social devotees. A few key drives assumed a critical part in the city's renaissance:

1. **Rebuilding and Conservation**
   The rebuilding and conservation of notable structures turned into a first concern. Talented skilled workers and conservators were utilized to fix and redesign frontier structures. This included reestablishing complicated façades, wooden overhangs, and yards to their previous brilliance.

2. **Foundation and Availability**
   To address gridlock and contamination, the city put resources into modernizing foundation. Passerby zones were made in pieces of the downtown area, and endeavors were made to work on open transportation and stopping offices. This upgraded the guest experience as well as worked on the personal satisfaction for occupants.

3. **Social Advancement**
   Social advancement assumed a huge part in Oaxaca's renewal. Celebrations and far-reaching developments were coordinated to commend the city's legacy. The Museo de las Culturas de Oaxaca, housed in the Santo Domingo complex, turned into a social community that displayed the city's set of experiences and customs.

4. **Local area Commitment**
   Connecting with the nearby local area was urgent to the rejuvenation endeavors. Native craftsmans were upheld in safeguarding and advancing their customary specialties. Drives were additionally sent off to enable native ladies financially through create cooperatives.

5. **The travel industry The board**

The travel industry, a crucial industry for Oaxaca, was made do with care. Reasonable the travel industry rehearses were elevated to guarantee that the inundation of guests didn't hurt the city's delicate social and ecological equilibrium. This included drives to lessen plastic waste and protect the city's regular environmental elements.

Achievement and Continuous Difficulties

The renewal of Oaxaca's Noteworthy Center has yielded huge victories:

Social Renaissance: The city's social legacy has encountered a renaissance. Oaxaca's notable structures, dynamic business sectors, and creative practices have drawn in sightseers and social lovers from around the world.

Financial Development: The renewal endeavors have prompted monetary development, helping nearby organizations and craftsmans. Oaxaca's customary specialties, including materials and earthenware, have earned worldwide respect.

Social Pride: The people group driven approach has imparted a feeling of social pride among inhabitants. Native customs have been praised and safeguarded, and the city's different populace exists together amicably.

Maintainable The travel industry: Oaxaca's way to deal with manageable the travel industry has guaranteed that the city's normal environmental elements, including the close by Monte Albán archeological site, stay safeguarded and available to people in the future.

In any case, challenges remain:

Feasible Development: Overseeing the travel industry development while protecting Oaxaca's social and ecological trustworthiness is a continuous test. Finding some kind of harmony between financial turn of events and protection is pivotal.

Framework Support: Progressing upkeep of foundation and memorable structures is fundamental to guarantee their drawn out protection.

Local area Strengthening: Proceeded with endeavors to engage native networks and save their conventional artworks are imperative for the city's social variety.

Worldwide Difficulties: Outside factors, including financial vacillations and worldwide occasions like the Coronavirus pandemic, can affect Oaxaca's travel industry and monetary soundness.

6.5 The importance of community involvement.

The Significance of Local area Association in Legacy Safeguarding

Local area inclusion is the foundation of fruitful legacy safeguarding endeavors all over the planet. Whether it's shielding notable milestones, safeguarding normal ponders, or reviving social fortunes, drawing in nearby networks is fundamental for guaranteeing the drawn out maintainability and progress of conservation drives. In this investigation, we will dig into the significant significance of local area contribution in legacy safeguarding.

Cultivating a Feeling of responsibility and Pride

At the point when networks are effectively participated in legacy conservation, they foster a feeling of responsibility and pride in their social and normal resources. These resources become basic pieces of their character, and inhabitants assume the job of stewards, guaranteeing that these fortunes are passed down to people in the future. This deep satisfaction inspires people to safeguard their legacy as well as encourages serious areas of strength for a guarantee to its protection.

Neighborhood Information and Skill

Networks have important neighborhood information and skill about their legacy destinations. This information incorporates customary structure procedures, social practices, and verifiable stories that may not be archived somewhere else.

At the point when networks are involved, this information is shared, saved, and integrated into protection procedures. This collaboration between neighborhood ability and conservation endeavors upgrades the realness and honesty of legacy destinations.

Maintainable Legacy The travel industry

Numerous legacy destinations depend on the travel industry for financial food. Local area contribution in the travel industry the board is urgent for guaranteeing that the convergence of guests is reasonable and conscious of nearby practices and the climate. Connected with networks can assist with finding some kind of harmony between advancing the travel industry and safeguarding the remarkable person of their legacy destinations. They can likewise benefit monetarily from the travel industry, adding to the general prosperity of the local area.

Compelling Protection Practices

Neighborhood people group frequently have a personal stake in the prosperity of their nearby environmental elements. They can act as careful overseers, detailing any indications of crumbling, defacement, or infringement on legacy destinations. This proactive contribution helps with early mediation, which is fundamental for forestalling irreversible harm. Furthermore, people group can partake in preservation endeavors, adding to the actual upkeep and rebuilding of legacy locales.

Social Recovery and Transmission

Conservation isn't just about actual designs; it's tied in with defending living customs and social practices. Drawing in networks in legacy safeguarding rejuvenates conventional specialties, music, dance, and other social articulations. It guarantees that these social fortunes are passed down to more youthful ages, forestalling their vanishing and adding to the dynamic quality of social legacy.

Enabling Nearby Economies

Legacy conservation can financially affect neighborhood networks. Reclamation projects make occupations, animate monetary action, and lift property estimations nearby legacy locales. By effectively taking part in safeguarding drives, networks can receive the monetary rewards while likewise guaranteeing the supported engaging quality of their region.

Inclusivity and Social Attachment

Drawing in networks in legacy safeguarding advances inclusivity and social union. It urges different gatherings to meet up, encouraging a feeling of solidarity and common perspective. This inclusivity rises above social, generational, and financial limits, advancing a more amicable society.

Difficulties and Contemplations

While people group association in legacy protection is foremost, it accompanies its own arrangement of difficulties and contemplations:

Adjusting Interests: Different people group individuals might have shifting interests and needs. Adjusting the necessities of different partners can be perplexing yet is fundamental for effective conservation.

Limit Building: People group might need help, preparing, and assets to take part in protection endeavors effectively. Limit building drives can assist with enabling networks.

Maintainability: Guaranteeing that local area association is supported over the long run is significant. This requires continuous commitment, correspondence, and a promise to shared objectives.

Regarding Native Privileges: In cases including native networks, it is fundamental to regard their freedoms, customary information, and independence in conservation endeavors.

The travel industry The board: While legacy the travel industry can bring financial advantages, it likewise presents difficulties connected with over-the travel industry and its effects on the climate and nearby culture. Mindful the travel industry the board is fundamental.

CHAPTER 7

Beyond the Wonders: Cultural Exchange

Past the Miracles: Social Trade and the Force of Legacy

Social trade is a unique interaction that rises above borders, improves social orders, and extends how we might interpret the world's different societies. It is a strong method for cultivating common regard, spanning separates, and praising the common legacy of mankind. While UNESCO's Reality Legacy Locales are in many cases the central marks of social trade, this peculiarity reaches out a long ways past these notable tourist spots. In this investigation, we will dive into the multi-layered domain of social trade, its importance, and the way that it stretches out past the marvels of the world.

Social Trade: An Impetus for Understanding

Social trade includes the collaboration, sharing, and mixing of social components, including customs, craftsmanship, music, cooking, language, and that's just the beginning. It fills in as a scaffold between social orders, working with grasping, sympathy, and the acknowledgment of our normal mankind. Past simple style or ceremonies, social trade offers significant bits of knowledge into the qualities, convictions, and yearnings of various societies. It challenges generalizations, separates hindrances, and makes the way for authentic exchange and participation.

1. **Social Discretion:** Social trade is a type of delicate strategy that empowers countries to draw in with each other on a more profound level. It advances culturally diverse comprehension and can add to compromise and peacebuilding. Nations frequently utilize social strategy to grandstand their way of life and values, encouraging altruism and participation.

2. **Saving Social Variety:** Social trade helps safeguard and praise the world's rich social variety. By drawing in with different societies, people and networks can find out about and value the uniqueness of each culture while perceiving the widespread components that associate all of us.

3. **Cultivating Resistance:** Openness to assorted societies through trade projects can advance resilience and battle bias and separation. It permits people to challenge their biases and foster a more open and comprehensive perspective.

4. **Monetary Advantages:** Social trade can animate the travel industry, exchange, and financial turn of events. The trading of merchandise, administrations, and imaginative manifestations frequently goes with social associations, helping neighborhood economies and setting out open doors for craftsmen and business people.

UNESCO World Legacy Locales as Social Government offices

UNESCO World Legacy Locales are fortunes of social and regular importance as well as act as representatives of culture and history. These notorious tourist spots draw in guests from around the world and become central focuses for social trade. They address mankind's common legacy and give a stage to culturally diverse exchange and understanding.

1. **Gaining from the Past:** World Legacy Locales offer looks into the existences of antiquated developments and the verifiable settings that formed them. Guests can find out about the engineering accomplishments, imaginative articulations, and social designs of these social orders.

2. **Diverse Commitment:** These locales frequently have worldwide occasions, displays, and instructive projects that work with multifaceted commitment. They act as scenes for specialists, researchers, and vacationers to interface and offer their points of view.

3. **Preservation and Maintainability:** The insurance and protection of World Legacy Destinations include global participation and backing. Endeavors to shield these locales frequently incorporate limit building and information trade among nations.

4. **Motivation for Innovativeness:** World Legacy Locales have propelled specialists, authors, and makers from the beginning of time. They give a wellspring of motivation to narrating, creative articulation, and social development.

Past the Marvels: Regular Social Trade

While UNESCO World Legacy Locales are critical center points of social trade, the pith of this peculiarity lies in regular communications, whether they happen in a clamoring market, a local eatery, or a local area occasion. Regular social trade envelops many exercises and encounters that advance comprehension and enthusiasm for assorted societies.

1. **Culinary Pleasures:** Food is a general language that rises above borders. Encountering the kinds of various foods permits people to interface with the set of experiences, customs, and culinary advancements of different societies.

2. **Language and Correspondence:** Learning another dialect or vernacular is a strong type of social trade. It encourages correspondence and compassion, empowering people to connect all the more profoundly with different societies.

3. **Celebrations and Festivities:** Going to celebrations, functions, and festivities in various societies offers knowledge into their practices, values, and social ceremonies. These occasions frequently welcome untouchables to take part, encouraging a feeling of local area and shared festival.

4. **Craftsmanship and Imagination:** Creative articulations, whether as music, dance, visual expressions, or writing, are vehicles for social trade. Craftsmen draw motivation from different societies, and their work can summon feelings and stories that reverberate across borders.

5. **Travel and Investigation:** Going to new spots and drawing in with neighborhood networks permits people to encounter social trade firsthand. It opens them to various lifestyles, challenges previously established inclinations, and widens their points of view.

The Computerized Age: Another Outskirts for Social Trade

In the computerized age, social trade has risen above actual limits, on account of innovation and the web. Online stages and web-based entertainment have made virtual spaces where individuals from around the world can interface, share, and find out about various societies.

1. **Virtual Social Encounters:** Computer generated reality (VR) and expanded reality (AR) innovations offer vivid social encounters, permitting clients to investigate legacy destinations, historical centers, and workmanship displays from their homes.

2. **Online Entertainment and Worldwide People group:** Web-based entertainment stages empower people to draw in with worldwide networks, trade thoughts, and gain from each other. Social powerhouses and content makers assume a part in sharing social bits of knowledge and customs.

3. **Online Training:** Online courses, online classes, and instructive assets have made it simpler for individuals to find out about different societies, dialects, and customs from the solace of their homes.

4. **Computerized Narrating:** The computerized age has democratized narrating, permitting people and networks to share their accounts, customs,

and encounters with a worldwide crowd through web journals, digital recordings, and recordings.

Difficulties and Contemplations

While social trade is an integral asset for cultivating understanding and appreciation, it isn't without its difficulties and contemplations:

1. **Social Allocation:** Social trade ought to continuously be conscious and delicate to the way of life included. It is fundamental to stay away from social assignment, which can prompt damage and deception.
2. **Power Elements:** In certain examples, social trade can sustain power awkward nature, with predominant societies affecting and eclipsing less favored ones. Endeavors ought to be made to guarantee fair trades.
3. **Commercialization:** Social trade can in some cases become popularized, with customary practices or relics took advantage of for benefit. Moral contemplations are important to forestall abuse.
4. **Safeguarding Native Freedoms:** While drawing in with native societies, it is vital for regard their privileges, including licensed innovation privileges, and include native networks in dynamic cycles.

7.1 The role of World Heritage Sites in fostering global cultural exchange.

The Job of World Legacy Destinations in Encouraging Worldwide Social Trade

UNESCO World Legacy Destinations possess an exceptional spot in the domain of social trade. These extraordinary tourist spots, perceived for their remarkable widespread worth, act as strong impetuses for cultivating worldwide social trade. They are not only images of a solitary country's legacy; they have a place with all of mankind and proposition a stage for discourse, understanding, and enthusiasm for the world's different societies. In this investigation, we will dig into the significant job that World Legacy Locales play in working with social trade on a worldwide scale.

World Legacy Locales as Junction of Culture

World Legacy Locales are the encapsulation of social and normal fortunes that have risen above topographical and fleeting limits. They address the climax of human inventiveness, creativity, and adoration for the climate. Past their inborn worth, these destinations are magnets for social trade because of a few key elements:

1. **All inclusiveness and Inclusivity:** World Legacy Locales have a place with all of humankind. They are articulations of our common history,

values, and desires. This all inclusiveness makes a feeling of having a place that rises above public boundaries and supports individuals from different foundations to interface with and gain from these destinations.

2. **Symbols of Social Variety:** These destinations address a kaleidoscope of societies, customs, and narratives. From the Pyramids of Egypt to the Incomparable Mass of China, they typify the exceptional attributes of their particular districts while featuring the consistent ideas that join human progress.

3. **Instructive Focuses:** World Legacy Destinations are not static relics but rather living instructive focuses. They offer open doors for guests to acquire bits of knowledge into the traditions, engineering, craftsmanship, and cultural designs of over a significant time span societies. Through directed visits, galleries, and shows, guests can develop how they might interpret the world's social extravagance.

4. **Stages for Exchange:** World Legacy Locales frequently have global meetings, workshops, and far-reaching developments. These social occasions unite specialists, researchers, and fans from different nations to take part in discourse, trade information, and team up on conservation endeavors.

Encouraging Social Trade: How World Legacy Destinations Make it happen

1. **The travel industry and Guest Commitment:** World Legacy Destinations draw in huge number of guests every year. These vacationers, addressing different identities, foundations, and interests, meet at these destinations, establishing a unique climate for social trade. Cooperations with local people, directed visits, and the trading of stories and encounters add to a rich embroidery of social commitment.

2. **Multifaceted Discoursed:** World Legacy Locales oftentimes have global gatherings, studios, and conferences. These occasions give a stage to researchers, specialists, and policymakers to participate in culturally diverse discoursed, share research discoveries, and team up on protection and preservation drives.

3. **Advancement of Theoretical Social Legacy:** Numerous World Legacy Destinations are personally associated with immaterial social legacy, like customary music, dance, and ceremonies. These living articulations of culture are frequently exhibited at the destinations, permitting guests to encounter the liveliness of neighborhood customs and cultivating an appreciation for the immaterial parts of legacy.

4. **Social The travel industry and Nearby Economies:** The financial advantages of the travel industry related with World Legacy Destinations can

be significant.

Neighborhood people group frequently benefit from expanded monetary open doors, including the offer of artworks, conventional food varieties, and directed visits. This monetary commitment further energizes social trade.

5. **Instructive Projects:** Instructive establishments and associations utilize World Legacy Destinations as open air study halls. Understudies and instructors visit these destinations to upgrade how they might interpret history, geology, nature, and social variety. This experiential learning adds to a worldwide point of view and enthusiasm for various societies.

6. **Virtual Access and Advanced Commitment:** In the computerized age, numerous World Legacy Locales offer virtual access through web-based visits, 3D reproductions, and media assets. These advanced drives extend the compass of social trade by permitting individuals from around the world to investigate and find out about these destinations from their own homes.

Contextual analyses in Social Trade through World Legacy Locales

1. **Machu Picchu, Peru:** This Inca fortification, an UNESCO World Legacy Site, draws in guests from all sides of the globe. It fills in as an image of old Inca culture and designing ability. Machu Picchu's notoriety has prompted diverse associations among travelers and nearby networks, encouraging comprehension and appreciation for Andean culture.

2. **Petra, Jordan:** The archeological site of Petra, known for its stone cut design, fills in as a scaffold among old and contemporary societies. Guests from around the world come to investigate this desert city, draw in with nearby Bedouin people group, and find out about the rich history of the district.

3. **Venice, Italy:** Venice's memorable city and tidal pond are not simply famous World Legacy Locales; they are likewise dynamic social communities. The Venice Biennale, a universally famous expressions presentation, is facilitated in the city and draws in craftsmen, keepers, and workmanship fans from assorted foundations. It fills in as a center point for creative trade and development.

4. **Galápagos Islands, Ecuador:** The Galápagos Islands, a World Legacy Site and a living research center of development, draw researchers and nature fans from around the world. Research stations on the islands work with worldwide logical cooperation and information trade in the areas of science and preservation.

Difficulties and Contemplations

While World Legacy Destinations assume a crucial part in cultivating social trade, certain difficulties and contemplations should be addressed to expand their true capacity:

1. **Overtourism:** The notoriety of some World Legacy Destinations has prompted issues of congestion and ecological corruption. Adjusting the craving for social trade with maintainable the travel industry rehearses is a basic test.
2. **Protection and Preservation:** The expanded appearance and human cooperation with these destinations can present conservation challenges. Finding some kind of harmony between guest commitment and site assurance is a continuous concern.
3. **Social Awareness:** Social trade ought to continuously be deferential and delicate to neighborhood customs, customs, and values. Guests should be taught about the significance of social regard and dependable the travel industry.
4. **Neighborhood Commitment:** Guaranteeing that nearby networks benefit from social trade related with World Legacy Locales is fundamental. Incorporation, financial open doors, and a feeling of responsibility are basic for their dynamic commitment.

7.2 Examples of international collaborations and partnerships.
Instances of Global Coordinated efforts and Organizations

In our undeniably interconnected world, global coordinated efforts and organizations have become fundamental vehicles for tending to worldwide difficulties, progressing logical examination, advancing monetary turn of events, and cultivating social trade. These coordinated efforts unite countries, associations, and people to pool assets, share ability, and all in all work toward shared objectives. In this investigation, we will dig into various models across various spaces that feature the power and effect of global joint efforts and associations.

Logical Undertakings

1. **The Huge Hadron Collider (LHC):** Situated at CERN (the European Association for Atomic Exploration) on the boundary among Switzerland and France, the LHC is the world's biggest and most impressive atom smasher. It includes commitments from north of 10,000 researchers and designers from in excess of 100 nations. The LHC has prompted momentous disclosures in molecule material science, remembering the affirmation of the Higgs boson for 2012.

2. **The Worldwide Space Station (ISS):** The ISS is an image of global participation in space investigation. It includes space offices from the US (NASA), Russia (Roscosmos), Europe (ESA), Japan (JAXA), and Canada (CSA). Space travelers from different countries live and cooperate on the station, directing logical exploration and examinations that benefit mankind.

3. **The Human Genome Venture:** This milestone project planned to guide and succession every one of the qualities of the human genome. It was a global exertion including researchers and organizations from the US, the Unified Realm, France, Germany, Japan, and China. The venture's fruitful culmination in 2003 has changed hereditary qualities and medication. Natural Preservation

4. **The Paris Understanding:** The Paris Arrangement, embraced in 2015, is a worldwide work to battle environmental change. It has been sanctioned by 189 nations and the European Association. Signatories focus on restricting an Earth-wide temperature boost to well under 2 degrees Celsius above pre-modern levels and seeking after endeavors to restrict it to 1.5 degrees Celsius. The understanding embodies worldwide cooperation to address a basic worldwide test.

5. **The Antarctic Settlement Framework:** The Antarctic Deal, endorsed in 1959, lays out Antarctica as a zone of harmony and collaboration for logical exploration. It has been endorsed by 54 nations and cultivates worldwide logical coordinated effort in Antarctica. The Madrid Convention, a correction to the settlement, assigns Antarctica as a characteristic save, safeguarding its exceptional climate.

6. **The Worldwide Sea Noticing Framework (GOOS):** GOOS is a worldwide cooperation that arranges worldwide endeavors to notice and screen the world's seas. It includes associations between nations, associations, and establishments to gather and share information on sea conditions, supporting logical examination and reasonable marine administration. General Wellbeing and Infectious prevention

7. **The Worldwide Polio Annihilation Drive:** Drove by the World Wellbeing Association (WHO), Turning Global, UNICEF, the CDC, and the Bill and Melinda Entryways Establishment, this drive plans to kill polio around the world. It includes cooperation with states, medical care laborers, and networks in impacted locales. Critical headway has been made, with a couple of nations detailing instances of wild poliovirus.

8. **The Admittance to Coronavirus Devices (ACT) Gas pedal:** Sent off in 2020, the Demonstration Gas pedal is a worldwide cooperation to speed up the turn of events, creation, and fair dispersion of Coronavirus tests, medicines, and immunizations. It unites state run administrations, worldwide associations, humanitarian establishments, and drug organizations

to battle the pandemic.

Financial Turn of events and Exchange

9. **The European Association (EU):** The EU is a great representation of territorial financial incorporation and cooperation. It contains 27 European nations that participate on different fronts, including exchange, financial arrangement, and security.

   The EU single market works with the free development of products, administrations, capital, and individuals, helping financial development and steadiness.

10. **The Transoceanic Organization (TPP):** Albeit the US pulled out from the TPP, it stays a critical illustration of worldwide exchange cooperation. The arrangement includes 11 nations in the Asia-Pacific locale and expects to decrease exchange obstructions and advance monetary mix.

    Social Trade and Legacy Protection

11. **UNESCO World Legacy:** UNESCO's Reality Legacy program is a worldwide work to safeguard and protect social and normal legacy locales of remarkable widespread worth. Nations team up to assign, make due, and monitor these locales, guaranteeing their conservation for people in the future. World Legacy Destinations represent global participation in social legacy.

12. **Global Social Celebrations:** Occasions like the Edinburgh Celebration Periphery in Scotland, the Cannes Film Celebration in France, and the Venice Biennale in Italy draw in craftsmen, entertainers, and crowds from around the world. These celebrations advance multifaceted trade, innovativeness, and the festival of different imaginative articulations.

    Helpful Guide and Improvement

13. **The Unified Countries (UN):** The UN is a transcendent illustration of worldwide cooperation in tending to helpful and improvement challenges. Its organizations, including UNICEF, UNHCR, and the World Food Program, work across boundaries to give help, support outcasts, and advance reasonable improvement objectives.

14. **Specialists Without Lines (Médecins Sans Frontières):** This global philanthropic association gives clinical consideration and help to individuals impacted by catastrophes, clashes, and scourges. It works in more than 70 nations, exhibiting the force of worldwide cooperation in medical services.

    Instruction and Scholarly Associations

15. **Erasmus+ Program:** The Erasmus+ program is an EU drive that upholds global intellectual and instructive trades. It empowers understudies, educators, and staff to study, educate, and train abroad, advancing social trade and cooperation in advanced education.

16. **Worldwide Exploration Joint efforts:** Colleges and examination foundations overall team up on logical examination projects, from environment demonstrating and space investigation to clinical revelations. These organizations improve information sharing, development, and the progression of human getting it.

Difficulties and Contemplations

While global coordinated efforts and associations offer huge advantages, they likewise accompany difficulties and contemplations:

1. **Various Interests:** Teaming up nations or associations might have assorted interests, needs, and goals. Adjusting these interests can be complicated and require discretion and exchange.
2. **Asset Allotment:** Cooperative endeavors frequently include asset portion and subsidizing circulation. Guaranteeing fair commitments and advantages can be a test.
3. **Lawful and Administrative Contrasts:** Different legitimate structures and guidelines across nations can present hindrances to coordinated effort. It is fundamental to Blend legitimate and administrative angles.
4. **Manageability:** Guaranteeing the drawn out maintainability of cooperative drives, particularly with regards to advancement and natural preservation, is pivotal.
5. **Social Awareness:** Social contrasts should be regarded and perceived to forestall errors or clashes during coordinated efforts, particularly in social trade and legacy safeguarding.

7.3 The cultural and economic impact of tourism.
The Social and Monetary Effect of The travel industry

The travel industry is a diverse industry that significantly affects both the social legacy and the monetary prosperity of objections all over the planet. It can possibly improve and protect social legacy while contributing fundamentally to neighborhood economies. Be that as it may, the effect of the travel industry isn't without its difficulties and contemplations. In this investigation, we will dive into the social and monetary components of the travel industry, analyzing the two its advantages and possible disadvantages.
Social Effect of The travel industry

1. **Social Trade and Enhancement:**
   The travel industry fills in as a scaffold for social trade, permitting individuals from different foundations to cooperate and gain from each other. Sightseers have the potential chance to drench themselves in

neighborhood customs, dialects, foods, and ways of life, encouraging shared understanding and appreciation. This social trade can prompt the protection and renewal of native practices and customs.

2. **Legacy Safeguarding:**
The travel industry frequently assumes an essential part in protecting social legacy. Famous vacationer locations every now and again put resources into the reclamation and upkeep of noteworthy locales, landmarks, and social tourist spots. The income produced from the travel industry can finance legacy protection endeavors, guaranteeing that these fortunes are passed down to people in the future.

3. **Advancing Social Mindfulness:**
The travel industry can bring issues to light about the significance of social variety and the need to safeguard it. Guests who draw in with neighborhood culture are bound to become advocates for social conservation and take part in dependable the travel industry rehearses, for example, regarding holy destinations and supporting nearby craftsmans.

4. **Restoring Customary Expressions and Specialties:**

The interest for credible social encounters can restore conventional expressions and artworks that could have in any case blurred into lack of definition. Neighborhood craftsmans frequently track down a business opportunity for their manifestations among travelers, empowering the continuation of customary craftsmanship.

Financial Effect of The travel industry

1. **Work Creation:**
The travel industry is a critical wellspring of work in numerous districts. It gives occupations in the friendliness and the travel industry areas as well as in related businesses, for example, transportation, food administrations, and retail. In certain networks, the travel industry is the essential type of revenue.

2. **Monetary Expansion:**
The travel industry can expand neighborhood economies, lessening reliance on a solitary industry. This broadening can make locales stronger to financial slumps in different areas.

3. **Framework Advancement:**
The deluge of sightseers frequently requires enhancements in framework, including streets, air terminals, and public transportation. These ventures benefit the two sightseers and nearby inhabitants by improving openness and personal satisfaction.

4. **Unfamiliar Trade Income:**

The travel industry can produce significant unfamiliar trade profit for nations. Guests burn through cash on convenience, food, transportation, and gifts, adding to a positive equilibrium of installments.

Difficulties and Contemplations

1. **Over-The travel industry:**
   Over-the travel industry happens when objections are overpowered by unnecessary quantities of sightseers, prompting ecological debasement, congestion, and stress on neighborhood assets. This can dissolve the exceptionally social and regular resources that draw in vacationers in any case.
2. **Social Commodification:**
   The commercialization of culture can prompt inauthentic encounters and the double-dealing of social practices and customs for benefit. Finding some kind of harmony between financial advantages and social authenticity is fundamental.
3. **Improvement:**
   The convergence of sightseers can drive up property costs and lead to the removal of neighborhood occupants, a peculiarity known as improvement. This can disturb networks and modify the social texture of an objective.
4. **Natural Effect:**
   The travel industry can have a huge ecological effect, including contamination, territory obliteration, and abuse of regular assets. Supportable the travel industry rehearses and dependable natural administration are significant for relieving these impacts.
5. **Occasional Work:**

In some vacationer locations, business amazing open doors are exceptionally occasional, prompting underemployment during off-busy times. This can bring about monetary shakiness for neighborhood inhabitants.

Feasible The travel industry as an Answer

Feasible the travel industry looks to expand the positive effect of the travel industry while limiting its adverse consequences. It includes capable travel rehearses, ecological protection, and local area commitment. Here are a few vital standards of feasible the travel industry:

1. **Local area Inclusion:**
   Connecting with neighborhood networks in the travel industry arranging and navigation guarantees that their advantages are thought of. It

additionally enables networks to take part in and benefit from the travel industry effectively.

2. **Protection and Safeguarding:**
Manageable the travel industry focuses on the security of regular and social legacy. This incorporates limiting the ecological impression of the travel industry and carrying out protection measures.

3. **Dependable The travel industry:**
Travelers are urged to embrace capable practices, for example, regarding neighborhood customs, limiting waste, and supporting nearby organizations. Visit administrators and facilities can likewise advance capable the travel industry.

4. **Financial Impartiality:**
Manageable the travel industry plans to circulate monetary advantages all the more impartially among neighborhood inhabitants. This might include fair wages, nearby obtaining, and local area venture.

5. **Objective Administration:**

Viable objective administration plans are significant for feasible the travel industry. These plans consider the conveying limit of an objective, foundation needs, and ecological effect evaluations.

Contextual analyses in Social and Monetary Effect

1. **Kyoto, Japan:**
Kyoto is eminent for its notable sanctuaries, places of worship, and conventional Japanese culture. The travel industry plays had a critical impact in saving Kyoto's social legacy by subsidizing the support and rebuilding of its noteworthy locales. Be that as it may, the city has confronted difficulties connected with over-the travel industry, prompting measures to oversee guest numbers and energize conscious way of behaving.

2. **Bhutan:**
Bhutan has embraced an exceptional way to deal with the travel industry by focusing on Gross Public Joy over GDP. The nation confines the quantity of travelers and requires a base everyday spend, which incorporates commitments to local area improvement and protection. This approach has helped safeguard Bhutan's way of life and climate.

3. **Barcelona, Spain:**
Barcelona has wrestled with the effects of over-the travel industry, including stuffing, rising lodging expenses, and clashes with nearby occupants. The city has executed measures to address these difficulties, for example, restricting the quantity of voyage transports and advancing elective attractions outside the downtown area.

4. Machu Picchu, Peru:

Machu Picchu is one of the most notorious vacationer locations universally, drawing in large number of guests yearly. While the travel industry has added to the conservation of this archeological miracle, it has additionally prompted worries about natural debasement and congestion. Specialists have acquainted guest amounts and guidelines with safeguard the site.

CHAPTER 8

Looking to the Future

Planning ahead: Exploring Difficulties and Embracing Potential open doors

What's in store is a unique scene formed by steadily developing patterns, advancements, and worldwide difficulties. As we look into the distance, it is fundamental to expect the progressions and improvements that lie ahead. In this investigation, we will look at key regions that will impact our aggregate future, the difficulties we face, and the open doors we should seize to fabricate a more reasonable, evenhanded, and versatile world.

1. **Innovative Headways and Computerized Change**

   The Ascent of Man-made reasoning (simulated intelligence) and Robotization:

   Man-made intelligence and robotization are ready to reshape enterprises, from assembling and medical services to back and instruction. While these advances offer effectiveness and development, they additionally bring up issues about work relocation and the requirement for new abilities and preparing.

   Advanced Consideration and Availability:

   Admittance to the web is turning out to be progressively basic for cooperation in the worldwide economy and society. Connecting the computerized partition and guaranteeing impartial admittance to advanced assets will be fundamental for tending to social and monetary inconsistencies.

   Network safety Difficulties:

   As computerized frameworks become more coordinated into our regular routines, the danger of cyberattacks develops. Safeguarding basic framework, individual information, and public safety will be principal in the advanced age.

2. **Environmental Change and Natural Maintainability**
   Speeding up Environment Activity:
   The criticalness of tending to environmental change is more clear than any time in recent memory. Countries, associations, and people should focus on lessening ozone harming substance emanations, progressing to sustainable power sources, and adjusting to a changing environment to stay away from devastating outcomes.
   Protection and Biodiversity:
   Safeguarding biodiversity and safeguarding environments is fundamental for the soundness of our planet. Preservation endeavors, maintainable horticulture, and capable land use are crucial parts of protecting the climate.
   Round Economy and Supportable Practices:
   The idea of a round economy, where assets are reused, reused, and reused, is picking up speed. Embracing supportable practices in assembling, utilization, and waste administration will be fundamental to diminishing ecological effect.

3. **Worldwide Wellbeing and Pandemic Readiness**
   Pandemic Flexibility:
   The Coronavirus pandemic has highlighted the requirement for strong worldwide wellbeing frameworks and pandemic readiness. Reinforcing medical care framework, immunization circulation, and early admonition frameworks will be fundamental to relieve future wellbeing emergencies.
   Emotional well-being Mindfulness:
   Emotional well-being difficulties, exacerbated by the pandemic, are getting expanded consideration. Lessening shame, growing admittance to emotional well-being administrations, and focusing on mental prosperity will be basic before very long.
   Worldwide Wellbeing Value:
   Guaranteeing evenhanded admittance to medical care and immunizations isn't just an ethical objective yet additionally significant for worldwide wellbeing security. Tending to variations in medical care conveyance and results is a complex however fundamental errand.

4. **Social and Social Changes**
   Variety and Consideration:
   It is a becoming cultural basic to Advance variety and consideration. Associations and networks should cultivate comprehensive conditions that celebrate variety and give equivalent open doors to all.
   Changing Work Examples:
   Remote work and adaptable work courses of action are changing the work environment. Adjusting the advantages of remote work with the requirement for in-person cooperation and resolving issues like balance between

serious and fun activities will be critical.

The Job of Training:

Schooling will assume a focal part in furnishing people with the abilities and information required for what's to come. Planning understudies for a quickly changing position market and encouraging decisive reasoning and flexibility will be fundamental.

5. **International Movements and Worldwide Relations**

Arising Worldwide Powers:

The worldwide international scene is developing, with the ascent of new worldwide powers and moving unions. Exploring these progressions and advancing tranquil discretion will be essential to worldwide dependability.

Helpful Emergencies and Movement:

Struggle, environmental change, and financial differences keep on driving helpful emergencies and relocation. Tending to these difficulties with sympathy and collaboration will be fundamental to safeguard weak populaces.

Network safety and Data Fighting:

As innovation propels, so do the dangers of cyberattacks and data fighting. Global cooperation and conciliatory endeavors will be important to address these dangers.

6. **Monetary Flexibility and Development**

Versatile Inventory Chains:

The pandemic uncovered weaknesses in worldwide stock chains. Constructing stronger and various inventory chains and decreasing dependence on single sources will be really important.

Supportable Monetary Development:

Offsetting financial development with supportability is a mind boggling challenge. Empowering advancement in clean advancements, environmentally friendly power, and maintainable practices will be basic.

Monetary Incorporation:

Advancing monetary incorporation and admittance to banking administrations for underserved populaces is a pathway to financial strengthening and destitution decrease.

7. **Administration and Moral Contemplations**

Moral computer based intelligence and Innovation:

As innovation propels, moral contemplations become more huge. Creating structures for mindful simulated intelligence and innovation use, including issues like information security and morals in man-made intelligence direction, will be basic.

Straightforwardness and Responsibility:

Reinforcing straightforwardness and responsibility in administration and corporate practices is fundamental for building trust and guaranteeing dependable authority.

Global Participation:
Worldwide difficulties require worldwide arrangements. Reinforcing global collaboration through associations like the Assembled Countries and territorial partnerships will be critical for resolving complex issues that rise above borders.

8. **Flexibility Notwithstanding Vulnerability**

Versatile Authority:
Pioneers in all areas should embrace versatility and ground breaking methodologies to explore vulnerability and drive positive change.

Local area Strength:
Networks assume an imperative part in strength. Building solid local area organizations and catastrophe readiness can upgrade strength at the nearby level.

Maintainable Ways of life:
People can add to a more maintainable future by embracing eco-accommodating works on, diminishing waste, and supporting moral and manageable organizations.

8.1 Emerging challenges in the preservation of world heritage.
Arising Difficulties in the Protection of World Legacy
Saving the world's social and regular legacy is a continuous undertaking that faces a large number of difficulties, both longstanding and arising. As our reality develops, new dangers and intricacies have arisen that influence the shielding of UNESCO World Legacy Destinations. In this investigation, we will dive into a portion of these arising provokes and consider procedures to address them.

1. **Environmental Change and Ecological Dangers**
Rising Ocean Levels and Seaside Disintegration:
Environmental change is prompting rising ocean levels, representing an immediate danger to seaside World Legacy Destinations. Notable areas like Venice and its tidal pond are especially defenseless against immersion, requiring inventive procedures for security.

Outrageous Climate Occasions:
More regular and extreme climate occasions, like tropical storms, floods, and out of control fires, jeopardize legacy destinations. Sufficient debacle readiness and environment versatile framework are fundamental to relieve these dangers.

Environment Disturbance:
Environmental change disturbs biological systems and influences the

greenery encompassing World Legacy Locales. Preservation endeavors should adjust to safeguard both the regular and social parts of these destinations.

2. **Over-The travel industry and Natural Effect**
Congestion and Debasement:
Numerous World Legacy Destinations are wrestling with over-the travel industry, prompting stuffing, harm to foundation, and ecological debasement. Carrying out guest the board plans and manageable the travel industry rehearses is pivotal.
Social Commodification:
The commercialization of culture at traveler objections can dissolve validness and lead to inauthentic encounters. Offsetting monetary advantages with social conservation is a mind boggling challenge.
Squander The board:
High guest numbers frequently bring about expanded squander age. Successful waste administration and reusing drives are expected to forestall contamination at legacy locales.

3. **Clashes and Equipped Struggle**
Struggle Zones:
World Legacy Destinations situated in struggle zones face the gamble of harm or obliteration. Clashes can disturb preservation endeavors and prevent access for observing and insurance.
Illegal Dealing:
Equipped struggles can fuel illegal dealing of social curios and artifacts, which further imperils social legacy. Fortifying regulations and worldwide participation is essential to battle this issue.

4. **Foundation Advancement and Urbanization**
Uncontrolled Urbanization:
Fast urbanization and framework improvement can infringe upon legacy destinations, modifying their environmental factors and sabotaging their uprightness. Hearty metropolitan arranging that considers legacy conservation is fundamental.
Transportation Development:
Transportation projects like air terminals and expressways can undermine the uprightness of legacy locales. Executing tough effect appraisals and taking into account elective courses can moderate these dangers.

5. **Advanced Difficulties**
Advanced Legacy Conservation:
While advanced innovations offer open doors for reporting and saving legacy, they additionally present difficulties connected with information capacity, legitimacy, and availability. It is basic to Foster advanced conservation methodologies.

Network safety Dangers:

The digitalization of legacy documentation and information presents network protection dangers. Safeguarding advanced documents from cyberattacks and guaranteeing information uprightness are squeezing concerns.

6. **Financial Tensions**

Improvement and Removal:

Monetary turn of events and the travel industry can prompt improvement, pushing nearby networks out of their notable areas. Finding some kind of harmony between legacy safeguarding and financial development is complicated yet vital.

Reasonableness of Preservation:

Safeguarding legacy destinations frequently accompanies significant expenses. Guaranteeing that preservation endeavors don't put an unnecessary monetary weight on have nations needs global help and subsidizing systems.

7. **Absence of Protection Abilities and Aptitude**

Abilities Hole:

Numerous areas come up short on fundamental mastery and assets for powerful legacy preservation. Limit building drives and information sharing are crucial for address this hole.

Preparing and Training:

Formal schooling and preparing programs in legacy protection are restricted in certain areas. Growing instructive open doors can support preservation endeavors.

8. **Moral and Legitimate Difficulties**

Bringing home and Possession:

Banters over bringing home of social curios and proprietorship freedoms can present moral and legitimate predicaments. Laying out clear rules for resolving these issues is critical.

Licensed innovation Freedoms:

The advanced period has brought up issues about protected innovation freedoms connected with legacy documentation and 3D reproductions. Settling these issues is fundamental for mindful legacy safeguarding.

9. **Pandemics and Wellbeing Concerns**

Effect of Wellbeing Emergencies:

Pandemics, similar to the Coronavirus pandemic, can disturb the travel industry, financing, and preservation endeavors. Systems for keeping up with legacy site security during wellbeing emergencies are required.

The travel industry Bounce back and Recuperation:

As the travel industry bounce back post-pandemic, offsetting monetary recuperation with legacy safeguarding is a sensitive errand. It is vital to Make arrangements for dependable the travel industry.

10. **The travel industry Patterns and Innovation**

Virtual The travel industry:

Headways in computer generated experience and expanded the truth are changing the way that vacationers draw in with legacy destinations. Guaranteeing that computerized encounters upgrade, as opposed to supplant, actual visits is a test.

Information Examination:

The travel industry information examination can illuminate guest the executives, yet there are moral worries about information protection and the effect of information driven choices on legacy destinations and neighborhood networks.

Tending to Arising Difficulties: Techniques and Arrangements

1. **Environment Strength and Transformation:**
   Put resources into environment versatile framework, early admonition frameworks, and preservation measures to shield legacy locales from ecological dangers.

2. **Practical The travel industry The executives:**
   Carry out economical the travel industry works on, including guest portions, instructive drives, and dependable travel rules, to relieve over-the travel industry.

3. **Struggle Alleviation:**
   Advance harmony and compromise to protect legacy destinations in struggle zones. Reinforce worldwide endeavors to battle unlawful dealing.

4. **Legacy Viable Metropolitan Preparation:**
   Integrate legacy protection into metropolitan preparation and foundation undertakings to guarantee the conjunction of legacy locales and metropolitan turn of events.

5. **Computerized Legacy Safeguarding:**
   Foster powerful advanced safeguarding systems, network protection measures, and worldwide norms for legacy digitization and information the executives.

6. **Limit Building and Instruction:**
   Put resources into legacy preservation schooling and limit working in locales with restricted mastery. Encourage information sharing and mentorship programs.

7. **Lawful Systems and Moral Rules:**
   Lay out clear lawful systems and moral rules for issues like bringing home, possession, and licensed innovation privileges.
8. **Pandemic Readiness:**
   Foster alternate courses of action for legacy site security during wellbeing emergencies and guarantee that recuperation methodologies balance financial and protection needs.
9. **Mindful The travel industry and Innovation:**
   Influence innovation for improved guest encounters while keeping up with the genuineness of legacy destinations. Guarantee mindful information use and protection in the travel industry the board.
10. **Global Joint effort:**

Advance global collaboration among state run administrations, associations, and networks to address arising difficulties on the whole.

Saving World Legacy Locales despite arising difficulties requires proactive procedures, global coordinated effort, and versatile methodologies. By perceiving the advancing idea of dangers to legacy and making a conclusive move, we can safeguard these important fortunes for people in the future and guarantee that they keep on rousing wonder and respect in a steadily impacting world.

8.2 Innovations and technologies aiding conservation efforts.

Developments and Advancements Helping Protection Endeavors

Preservation endeavors have been altogether improved by the coming of inventive innovations. These apparatuses engage moderates, analysts, and associations to screen, secure, and reestablish regular habitats and social legacy all the more successfully. In this investigation, we will dive into a few developments and advancements that are putting forth a huge effect on protection attempts.

1. **Remote Detecting and Satellite Imaging**
   LiDAR (Light Recognition and Going):
   LiDAR innovation utilizes laser heartbeats to make nitty gritty 3D guides of scenes and landscape. It is significant for evaluating woodland cover, planning archeological locales concealed underneath vegetation, and observing changes in geology because of elements like deforestation and disintegration.
   Satellite Imaging:
   Satellite symbolism gives a worldwide viewpoint on natural changes. High-goal satellite pictures can follow deforestation, screen the soundness of coral reefs, and identify unlawful logging exercises. These pictures likewise aid catastrophe the executives and untamed life following.

2. **Geographic Data Frameworks (GIS)**
   Spatial Information Investigation:
   GIS devices permit traditionalists to dissect spatial information and settle on informed conclusions about protection needs. These frameworks assist with recognizing basic territories, plan safeguarded regions, and evaluate the effect of human exercises on biological systems.
   Natural life Following:
   GIS is utilized to follow the developments of untamed life populaces, assisting analysts with understanding movement designs, territory use, and the effect of environmental change on creature conduct.

3. **Preservation Robots**
   Aeronautical Reconnaissance:
   Preservation drones or Automated Elevated Vehicles (UAVs) give a practical method for checking remote and out of reach regions. They are utilized for undertakings like enemy of poaching watches, untamed life overviews, and surveying the strength of biological systems from the air.

4. **DNA Examination and Hereditary Checking**
   DNA Barcoding:
   DNA barcoding permits researchers to recognize species rapidly and precisely by examining hereditary markers. It helps with distinguishing jeopardized species, following the beginnings of seized natural life items, and checking biodiversity.
   Genomic Sequencing:
   Genomic sequencing assists analysts with grasping the hereditary variety of populaces and species. This data is significant for preservation rearing projects, overseeing hereditary wellbeing, and saving jeopardized species.

5. **Man-made consciousness and AI**
   Camera Traps and Picture Acknowledgment:
   Man-made consciousness (simulated intelligence) and AI calculations are utilized to dissect immense measures of camera trap pictures and distinguish natural life species and ways of behaving. This innovation aids populace observing and hostile to poaching endeavors.
   Prescient Demonstrating:
   Artificial intelligence is utilized to foster prescient models for biological patterns, for example, the spread of intrusive species or the effect of environmental change on biological systems. These models illuminate preservation procedures and transformation plans.

6. **Shrewd Sensors and IoT (Web of Things)**
   Natural Observing:
   Brilliant sensors and IoT gadgets gather continuous information on natural boundaries like temperature, moistness, water quality, and air contamination. These information assist with following living space well-

being and the effect of environmental change.

Natural life Telemetry:
Scaled down GPS beacons, for example, GPS restraints and labels, permit analysts to screen the developments of creatures. This data supports understanding movement courses, natural surroundings use, and the way of behaving of imperiled species.

7. **Blockchain Innovation**
Production network Straightforwardness:
Blockchain innovation is utilized to make straightforward inventory chains for items like lumber, fish, and natural life items. This helps battle unlawful logging and the exchange imperiled species by giving obvious, carefully designed records.

8. **Computer generated Reality (VR) and Expanded Reality (AR)**
Virtual Protection Schooling:
VR and AR advancements empower virtual visits to normal and social legacy destinations. This can be utilized for instruction and mindfulness crusades, permitting individuals to encounter these locales from a distance and encouraging a feeling of association.

9. **Computerized Preservation Robots**
Coral Rebuilding:
Automated frameworks are utilized for coral reef reclamation by establishing coral parts and checking their development. These robots can cover huge regions rapidly and proficiently.

10. **Preservation Applications and Resident Science**
Natural life Checking Applications:
Portable applications permit residents to add to natural life checking endeavors by recording sightings and gathering information. This publicly supported information helps with grasping species appropriation and conduct.

Local area Commitment:
Applications and social stages assist with associating networks to preservation endeavors, bringing issues to light and encouraging neighborhood support in protection exercises.

11. **3D Printing and Replication**
Curio Replication:
3D printing innovation is utilized to imitate social curios, models, and building components. This helps protect legacy locales by lessening mileage from guest collaboration.

12. **Environment Demonstrating and Expectation**
Environmental Change Alleviation:
High level environment demonstrating devices help with anticipating the effect of environmental change on biological systems and species. This

data illuminates preservation techniques, like territory reclamation and helped movement.

13. **Water Sanitization and Territory Rebuilding Innovations**
Environmental Rebuilding:
Imaginative advancements for water sanitization and environment rebuilding help in cleaning contaminated water bodies, reestablishing wetlands, and restoring harmed biological systems.

14. **Sound Decrease and Territory Observing**
Clamor Hosing:
Sound decrease advancements limit aggravations in normal environments brought about by human exercises. This advantages natural life that is delicate to clamor contamination.
Bioacoustics:
Bioacoustic observing frameworks catch and break down sounds in common habitats. This helps track untamed life populaces and distinguish changes in biodiversity.

15. **Protection Advanced mechanics and Independent Vehicles**

Submerged Investigation:
Independent submerged vehicles (AUVs) and remotely worked vehicles (ROVs) help with investigating and observing marine biological systems, especially in remote ocean conditions.

Underground and Cavern Investigation:
Automated frameworks are utilized for cavern and underground living space investigation, which is frequently excessively risky for human analysts.

These advancements and innovations are upsetting protection endeavors across the globe. Nonetheless, it's fundamental to perceive that innovation alone isn't a panacea for protection challenges. Fruitful protection actually requires joint effort, strategy backing, financing, and neighborhood commitment. As innovation keeps on propelling, the collaboration among development and preservation will assume an essential part in safeguarding our normal and social legacy for people in the future.

8.3 The evolving role of UNESCO in the 21st century.
The Advancing Job of UNESCO in the 21st 100 years
The Unified Countries Instructive, Logical, and Social Association (UNESCO) was laid out in 1945 with a mission to advance worldwide coordinated effort in schooling, science, culture, and correspondence. Throughout the long term, UNESCO's job has advanced because of changing worldwide elements, arising difficulties, and the developing needs of part states. In the 21st 100 years, UNESCO keeps on assuming a crucial part in resolving complex worldwide

issues and encouraging global collaboration. Here, we investigate the developing job of UNESCO in hundred years.

1. **Training for All and Deep rooted Learning**

   One of UNESCO's fundamental missions is to guarantee quality training for all. In the 21st 100 years, this mission has taken on new aspects. UNESCO centers around admittance to essential instruction as well as on advancing long lasting learning open doors for individuals, all things considered. This incorporates endeavors to work on the nature of schooling, improve educator preparing, and encourage computerized proficiency.

   In a quickly impacting world, UNESCO perceives the significance of furnishing people with the abilities and information expected to adjust and flourish. Instruction is viewed as a foundation of maintainable turn of events, adding to destitution decrease, orientation balance, and social union.

2. **Safeguarding Social Legacy and Advancing Social Variety**

   UNESCO's obligation to protecting social legacy stays immovable, however the difficulties have developed. In the 21st 100 years, social legacy faces dangers from urbanization, globalization, furnished clashes, and environmental change. UNESCO assumes a urgent part in recognizing and safeguarding World Legacy Destinations, both normal and social, and in preparing global help for their preservation.

   Moreover, UNESCO advances social variety and intercultural exchange as a way to encourage resistance, harmony, and shared understanding. In a world set apart by social pluralism, UNESCO's work in safeguarding and advancing social articulations is more pertinent than any time in recent memory.

3. **Propelling Science, Innovation, and Development**

   The 21st century has seen remarkable advances in science and innovation, changing the manner in which we live and work. UNESCO perceives the focal job of science and development in tending to worldwide difficulties, from environmental change to wellbeing emergencies.

   UNESCO's part in this setting incorporates advancing logical collaboration, supporting exploration limit working in agricultural nations, and pushing for the moral utilization of logical disclosures. Moreover, UNESCO's Intergovernmental Oceanographic Bonus (IOC) is attempting to improve how we might interpret the world's seas and address issues like marine contamination and overfishing.

4. **Cultivating Opportunity of Articulation and Media Education**

   The computerized age has introduced new open doors for correspondence and articulation, yet it has likewise raised difficulties connected with the spread of disinformation, disdain discourse, and advanced separates.

UNESCO plays extended its part in advancing opportunity of articulation, media pluralism, and admittance to data.

Specifically, UNESCO advocates for media education to engage people to basically survey data sources and explore the advanced scene capably. The association additionally addresses dangers to columnists and supports press opportunity around the world.

5. **Tending to Worldwide Difficulties**

UNESCO's part in the 21st century reaches out to tending to complex worldwide difficulties that rise above borders. These incorporate environmental change, biodiversity misfortune, the computerized partition, and the assurance of basic liberties.

UNESCO's commitment to environment activity incorporates endeavors to safeguard normal World Legacy Locales, advance environment schooling, and backing environment strong practices in social and regular legacy protection. UNESCO likewise perceives the significance of saving etymological variety and conventional information notwithstanding ecological change.

6. **Advancing Orientation Correspondence and Consideration**

Orientation correspondence and the strengthening of ladies and young ladies are vital to UNESCO's central goal. The association attempts to guarantee equivalent admittance to schooling, advance orientation delicate educational programs, and advance ladies' cooperation in science, innovation, and social conservation.

UNESCO's drives additionally stretch out to consideration and the privileges of people with handicaps. The association advocates for open training, social foundations, and advanced stages to guarantee that all people can take part completely in the public eye.

7. **Reinforcing Global Collaboration**

In a profoundly interconnected world, UNESCO's part in working with global collaboration is principal. The association fills in as a stage for part states to team up on shared objectives, trade information and best practices, and prepare assets for basic drives.

UNESCO's meeting power is exemplified by its job in planning the Worldwide Training Alliance, an organization pointed toward guaranteeing instructive progression during the Coronavirus pandemic. Such endeavors show UNESCO's capacity to answer arising difficulties with dexterity and fortitude.

8. **Embracing Innovation and Development for UNESCO's Central goal**

In embracing the valuable open doors introduced by innovation, UNESCO has started advanced change endeavors to improve its work. This incorporates involving computerized instruments for schooling, social protection, and information assortment. UNESCO likewise investigates the capability of man-made consciousness (simulated intelligence) and information examination to actually address worldwide difficulties more.

UNESCO perceives the significance of saddling the Fourth Modern Unrest to propel its main goal while staying aware of moral contemplations, information protection, and computerized availability.

CHAPTER 9

Conclusion

Determination: Forming a Feasible and Comprehensive Future through UNESCO

All through this broad investigation of UNESCO's complex job in the 21st hundred years, it turns out to be unmistakably clear that the association remains at the very front of worldwide endeavors to shape a practical, comprehensive, and socially rich future for humankind. UNESCO's central goal, conceived out of the cinders of The Second Great War, has constantly advanced to address the steadily changing difficulties and chances of our times.

As we consider the different components of UNESCO's work — schooling, culture, science, correspondence, ecological preservation, orientation equity, and that's only the tip of the iceberg — we see an association that has adjusted as well as flourished in an undeniably interconnected and complex world. UNESCO has reliably shown its obligation to building harmony through the trading of information, the festival of social variety, and the advancement of basic freedoms.

A Guide of Instructive Advancement

Training lies at the core of UNESCO's central goal, and in the 21st hundred years, this responsibility has taken on new importance. UNESCO's work in guaranteeing comprehensive, quality schooling for everything is instrumental in decreasing imbalances, advancing financial turn of events, and cultivating worldwide citizenship.

In a time where mechanical headways and the computerized partition present the two difficulties and potential open doors, UNESCO's job in progressing advanced proficiency and evenhanded admittance to training couldn't possibly be more significant. The association's accentuation on long lasting learning recognizes that training is a deep rooted venture, one that furnishes people with the abilities expected to explore a consistently impacting world.

Watchmen of Social Legacy

Social legacy, both unmistakable and immaterial, is a demonstration of human imagination, history, and character. UNESCO's resolute obligation to protecting social legacy despite developing dangers —, for example, urbanization, environmental change, and furnished struggle — is essential. The association's endeavors to safeguard World Legacy Locales, protect social variety, and advance intercultural discourse are fundamental in a globalized world set apart by social pluralism.

UNESCO's devotion to cultivating the innovative enterprises, supporting craftsmen, and protecting native information frameworks guarantees that social legacy stays a living, unique power that enhances social orders and rises above borders.

Bosses of Logical Advancement

Science and innovation have the ability to address a portion of mankind's most squeezing difficulties, from environmental change to general wellbeing emergencies. UNESCO's part in progressing logical collaboration, supporting examination, and it is fundamental to advance moral logical practices.

In a period where logical revelations can possibly reshape our reality, UNESCO's accentuation on dependable science and the moral utilization of innovation is a directing light. The association's commitment to environment activity, sea investigation, and biodiversity protection epitomizes its obligation to supportable improvement through science and development.

Defenders of Opportunity of Articulation and Media Proficiency

The computerized age has introduced new wildernesses for correspondence and articulation. UNESCO's commitment to opportunity of articulation, media pluralism, and admittance to data has never been more appropriate. In reality as we know it where data can both enable and trick, UNESCO's support for media education engages people to basically evaluate data sources and explore the computerized scene capably.

The association's work in supporting writers, safeguarding press opportunity, and countering disdain discourse guarantees that the standards of a majority rule government and common liberties are maintained, even in the computerized domain.

Handling Worldwide Difficulties with Global Participation

UNESCO perceives that a significant number of the difficulties we face today — environmental change, biodiversity misfortune, the computerized gap, and that's just the beginning — require worldwide arrangements. The association fills in as a stage for worldwide participation, empowering part states to team up on shared objectives, trade information, and prepare assets.

UNESCO's ability to meet, coordinate, and prepare aggregate activity was particularly obvious during the Coronavirus pandemic, where it assumed a critical part in guaranteeing instructive coherence and supporting the most weak networks.

Advancing Orientation Uniformity and Consideration

Orientation uniformity and consideration are beliefs as well as objectives for supportable turn of events and harmony. UNESCO's endeavors to guarantee equivalent admittance to schooling, advance orientation delicate educational programs, and advance ladies' support in science, innovation, and social protection are essential strides toward a more evenhanded world.

By perceiving the significance of inclusivity and the privileges of people with inabilities, UNESCO cultivates a feeling of having a place and investment among all people, no matter what their experience or capacities.

Outfitting Innovation and Development for a Superior Tomorrow

In embracing the potential open doors introduced by innovation, UNESCO has set out on an excursion of computerized change. By utilizing computerized devices for schooling, social conservation, and information assortment, the association upgrades its effect in a quickly impacting world. UNESCO's investigation of man-made brainpower, information examination, and advanced availability highlights obligation to development serves humankind's wellbeing.

Planning ahead with Trust and Resolve

As we finish up this investigation of UNESCO's developing job in the 21st hundred years, we are reminded that the association isn't just an element yet an encouraging sign. UNESCO embodies the force of worldwide participation, social comprehension, and information trade to fabricate a superior future.

In a period set apart by complex difficulties — pandemics, environment emergencies, computerized upheavals, and international strains — UNESCO stays immovable in its main goal to assemble harmony in the personalities of people. Its work rises above borders, joins countries, and praises the lavishness of human variety.

UNESCO's excursion in the 21st century is one of transformation, strength, and immovable obligation to the beliefs of the Assembled Countries. As we plan ahead, we are helped to remember UNESCO's immortal message: that instruction, culture, science, and correspondence are the establishments whereupon we can build a universe of harmony, maintainability, and inclusivity.

UNESCO isn't simply an association; it is a living demonstration of the persevering through conviction that through information, discourse, and participation, we can defeat the difficulties within recent memory and fashion a way toward a more splendid, more amicable future.

The excursion proceeds, and with UNESCO driving the way, we face the future with trust and resolve, prepared to embrace the open doors that lie ahead.

9.1 Recap of the significance of UNESCO's World Heritage program.

Recap of the Meaning of UNESCO's Reality Legacy Program

The UNESCO World Legacy program, laid out in 1972, has turned into an image of worldwide collaboration and obligation to saving our planet's most valuable social and regular fortunes. All through this excursion, we have investigated the diverse meaning of this program, which stretches out a long ways past the simple assignment of notorious locales. As we recap the vital parts of its significance, obviously the World Legacy program fills in as a demonstration of the persevering through worth of our common legacy and the dire need to safeguard it for people in the future.

1. **Protecting Social and Normal Variety**
   At the core of the World Legacy program is the protection of the world's rich social and normal variety. By assigning locales as World Legacy, UNESCO perceives their remarkable worth to mankind. These locales address the aggregate memory of civilizations, the authority of human innovativeness, and the phenomenal magnificence of the regular world. The program guarantees that this variety isn't lost to the desolates of time, advancement, or struggle.

2. **Cultivating Global Collaboration and Fortitude**
   UNESCO's Reality Legacy program is a brilliant illustration of global participation and fortitude. It unites countries from across the globe to defend and praise our common legacy aggregately. The program rises above political, social, and topographical limits, cultivating a feeling of solidarity among countries in quest for a shared objective: the security of our reality's most remarkable spots.

3. **Advancing Manageable Turn of events**
   World Legacy Destinations are not just static relics of the past; they are no nonsense scenes that frequently support networks and economies. UNESCO perceives the significance of manageable improvement around these locales. This includes tracking down a fragile harmony between moderating the site's respectability and taking into consideration mindful the travel industry and nearby financial turn of events. Supportable practices at and around World Legacy Locales can act as models for mindful stewardship of our planet's assets.

4. **Improving Social Getting it and Discourse**
   World Legacy Destinations are windows into the assorted societies, customs, and chronicles that make up our reality. They offer open doors for social trade and shared understanding.
   By advancing these locales, UNESCO supports discourse and appreciation among various societies, cultivating admiration and resilience. In a world frequently set apart by division and struggle, this part of the program is an amazing asset for advancing harmony.

5. **Rousing Stunningness and Respect for Nature**
   The regular World Legacy Destinations, with their amazing scenes and novel environments, act as tokens of the unbelievable magnificence and delicacy of our normal world. They motivate wonder and adoration for

nature, helping us to remember our obligation to be stewards of the climate. In a period of natural difficulties like environmental change and biodiversity misfortune, these destinations act as encouraging signs and preservation.

6. **Social and Regular Miracles as Instructive Devices**

    World Legacy Destinations are important instructive assets. They offer open doors for experiential picking up, interfacing individuals — particularly the more youthful ages — with their social legacy and the regular world. These destinations give vivid illustrations ever, topography, environment, and that's only the tip of the iceberg. They invigorate interest, empower investigation, and cultivate a long lasting adoration for learning.

7. **Bringing issues to light of Conservation Difficulties**

    The World Legacy program likewise focuses a light on the difficulties of protection. Many locales face dangers, like contamination, poaching, urbanization, and environmental change. UNESCO's endeavors to screen and safeguard these destinations bring issues to light about the earnest requirement for protection. By featuring the battles looked by these famous spots, the program activates support for their insurance and the more extensive worldwide climate.

8. **Setting a High Bar for Safeguarding Guidelines**

    Assignment as a World Legacy Site accompanies a bunch of thorough safeguarding principles. Destinations should meet explicit measures connected with their excellent worth and honesty. This sets a high bar for protection and preservation endeavors, pushing nations and networks to focus on the defending of their social and regular fortunes.

9. **Observing Human Accomplishment and Normal Miracles**

    The World Legacy program is a festival of human accomplishment and the dazzling miracles of the regular world. It perceives the fantastic accomplishments of designing, engineering, and imagination that have molded our set of experiences. It likewise honors the exceptional powers of nature that have formed our planet over centuries. These destinations give a wellspring of motivation and pride for individuals all over the planet.

10. **Building an Inheritance for People in the future**

Maybe the most getting through meaning of the World Legacy program is its job in building a heritage for people in the future.

By safeguarding these excellent destinations today, we guarantee that our youngsters and grandkids can likewise encounter the miracle and excellence of our common legacy. The program encapsulates a promise to intergenerational value, passing down a world improved by culture and biodiversity.

9.2 The responsibility of current and future generations in preservation. The Obligation of Current and People in the future in Protection

Protection isn't exclusively the weight of the present; an obligation rises above time and ages. The custodianship of our planet's social and normal legacy is a common commitment that both current and people in the future should embrace. In this interconnected world, where the activities of one age influence the tradition of those to come, the meaning of this obligation couldn't possibly be more significant.

Overseers of Social Legacy

Social legacy is the vault of humankind's aggregate memory, imagination, and personality. From old landmarks and archeological destinations to fine arts, compositions, and customs, it typifies the social variety that makes our reality rich and lively. Saving social legacy isn't just a demonstration of stewardship yet additionally a promise to passing on the tales, values, and customs that shape our social orders.

1. **Defending Social Fortunes**
   Current ages bear the obligation of defending social fortunes for what's in store. This incorporates safeguarding World Legacy Locales, saving works of art and ancient rarities, and guaranteeing the endurance of jeopardized dialects and conventional practices. It requires interests in rebuilding, preservation, and social rejuvenation.
2. **Embracing Supportable Practices**
   Protection endeavors ought to line up with manageability standards. Reasonable the travel industry, for example, guarantees that social locales can be delighted in by people in the future without really hurting. It includes mindful guest the executives, supportable advancement around legacy destinations, and limiting the natural effect of the travel industry.
3. **Sending Information and Values**

Communicating information about social legacy to people in the future is critical. Schooling assumes a critical part in this cycle. By integrating social legacy into educational plans and advancing social mindfulness, social orders can guarantee that more youthful ages figure out the significance of conservation and feel a feeling of pride over their legacy.

Stewards of Regular Legacy

Normal legacy, incorporating environments, scenes, and biodiversity, is similarly essential for the prosperity of current and people in the future. These normal marvels give fundamental assets, support life on The planet, and add to our physical and mental prosperity. Saving them is a demonstration of self-protection for humankind.

1. **Biodiversity Protection**

    The obligation to moderate biodiversity falls soundly on the shoulders of current ages. This implies safeguarding imperiled species, saving environments, and moderating the effects of environmental change, living space obliteration, and contamination. Biodiversity misfortune influences food security, medication, and the equilibrium of our biological systems.

2. **Environment Activity**

    Tending to environmental change is a worldwide obligation shared by all ages. Current activities, from decreasing fossil fuel byproducts to changing to environmentally friendly power sources, have significant ramifications for the environment that people in the future will acquire. Environment activity today is an interest in a maintainable future.

3. **Reasonable Asset The board**

Reasonable asset the board is basic to guarantee that people in the future approach fundamental assets like clean water, rich soil, and solid woodlands. Impractical abuse of regular assets undermines the climate as well as compromises the prosperity of future social orders.

Adjusting Advancement and Conservation

One of the focal difficulties for current and people in the future is finding some kind of harmony among advancement and conservation. The requirement for financial advancement, foundation, and urbanization frequently conflicts with the basic to safeguard social and regular legacy. Finding creative arrangements that orchestrate these targets is fundamental.

1. **Economical Turn of events**

    The idea of economical advancement is vital in such manner. Feasible advancement tries to address the issues of the present without compromising the capacity of people in the future to address their own issues. It supports earth capable practices, fair monetary development, and social prosperity.

2. **Comprehensive Navigation**

Including different voices and viewpoints in direction is fundamental. This guarantees that advancement plans think about the interests and worries, everything being equal, including neighborhood networks, native people groups, and people in the future. Inclusivity cultivates a feeling of shared liability.

Utilizing Innovation for Conservation

Innovation assumes an extraordinary part in conservation endeavors. Current and people in the future should bridle mechanical advancements to upgrade preservation and address natural difficulties.

1. **Computerized Protection**
   The computerized age offers open doors for saving social legacy through digitization. Digitized records, craftsmanships, and authentic reports can be protected for people in the future. Also, advanced apparatuses help in checking and overseeing regular legacy.
2. **Ecological Innovations**

State of the art advancements like remote detecting, man-made consciousness, and enormous information examination help with checking and moderating natural dangers. These devices give significant bits of knowledge to preservation endeavors.

Instruction and Mindfulness
Training and mindfulness building are strong devices in connecting with current and people in the future in conservation endeavors. By imparting a feeling of obligation and appreciation for social and regular legacy, social orders can support an enduring obligation to protection.

1. **Instructive Educational programs**
   Remembering safeguarding and manageability for instructive educational programs furnishes understudies with the information and values vital for dependable citizenship. It encourages a comprehension of the interconnectedness between human exercises and the climate.
2. **Public Effort**

Public effort missions and mindfulness drives assume a basic part in connecting with networks. They energize dependable the travel industry, advance maintainable utilization, and rally public help for preservation measures.

Lawful Structures and Global Collaboration
Safeguarding endeavors require a hearty legitimate structure and worldwide participation. Peaceful accords, for example, the World Legacy Show and environment concurs, give an establishment to cooperative activity.

1. **Fortifying Legitimate Securities**
   Countries should reinforce legitimate assurances for social and normal legacy inside their locales. This incorporates instituting and authorizing regulations against unlawful untamed life exchange, social property robbery, and living space obliteration.
2. **Worldwide Associations**

Worldwide collaboration is irreplaceable in tending to worldwide difficulties like environmental change and biodiversity misfortune. Cooperative drives and arrangements empower countries to pool assets and ability for successful preservation.

Safeguarding as a Heritage and a Gift

Safeguarding is a heritage that ongoing ages can offer to what's in store. It is an endowment of history, culture, and the regular world. The obligation of conservation isn't a weight yet a chance to leave a positive engraving on the world.

1. **A Living Heritage**

   By effectively captivating in protection endeavors, current ages make a living heritage for people in the future. They guarantee that the miracles of our reality stay in one piece and keep on motivating amazement and marvel.
2. **An Ethical Objective**

Conservation isn't just a question of reasonability yet additionally an ethical goal. It mirrors our obligation to safeguard the climate and honor the social commitments of past ages.

9.3 Final thoughts on the enduring importance of the seven wonders of preservation.

Last Considerations on the Persevering through Significance of the Seven Marvels of Conservation

As we finish up our investigation of the Seven Marvels of Protection — UNESCO's Reality Legacy program and its significant effect on the preservation of social and normal fortunes — it is apparent that the significance of these miracles stretches out a long ways past their actual presence. They act as representative mainstays of our obligation to shielding the tradition of humankind and the planet. In these last considerations, we think about the persevering through meaning of these miracles and the obligations they present to us.

1. **Gatekeepers of Social and Regular Variety**

   The Seven Miracles of Protection address the watchmen of social and regular variety. They advise us that our reality is a mosaic of societies, customs, and environments, each with its remarkable excellence and worth. By saving these marvels, we recognize the significance of shielding the rich embroidered artwork of mankind's set of experiences and the unprecedented biodiversity that supports life on The planet.
2. **Demonstrations of Human Innovativeness and Regular Magnificence**

   These marvels are living demonstrations of the levels of human imagination and the remarkable glory of the normal world. They stand as proof of our ability to imagine, plan, and construct wonders that rise above time and motivate ages. In their presence, we are lowered by the accomplishments of our predecessors and the amazing excellence of our planet.

3. **Images of Worldwide Participation and Solidarity**

   The World Legacy program is a brilliant illustration of global collaboration and solidarity. These marvels are the consequence of aggregate endeavors to rise above political, social, and geological limits chasing a shared objective: the insurance of our common legacy. They act as images of what humankind can accomplish when countries cooperate for a higher reason.

4. **Training and Motivation for All Ages**

   The miracles are not static relics; they are living homerooms that teach and move individuals, everything being equal. They offer open doors for experiential getting the hang of, cultivating a long lasting adoration for investigation and disclosure. They help us that the pursuit to remember information exceeds all logical limitations and that social and regular miracles are the best educators.

5. **Impetuses for Practical Turn of events**

   Manageable improvement is at the core of the World Legacy program. These marvels are not segregated islands but rather basic pieces of networks and environments. They show the way that mindful improvement can coincide with protection, making a model for maintainable practices that can help social orders and economies without compromising the trustworthiness of these excellent destinations.

6. **Advertisers of Social Getting it and Harmony**

   In a world frequently set apart by divisions and clashes, these marvels advance social comprehension and harmony. They support exchange among assorted societies and encourage regard for various customs. They advise us that, underneath our disparities, we share a typical humankind and a typical home — the Earth.

7. **Tokens of Protection Difficulties and Obligations**

   The Seven Miracles of Protection are not insusceptible to dangers. They are presented to environmental change, urbanization, contamination, poaching, and different difficulties. Their weakness fills in as an unmistakable sign of the obligations we bear to safeguard them. These miracles force us to make a move, bring issues to light, and prepare assets to address the squeezing protection issues within recent memory.

8. **Motivations for People in the future**

   Maybe their most getting through importance lies in the motivation they give to people in the future.

   These miracles light interest, fuel dreams, and urge youthful personalities to imagine a future where safeguarding and progress remain forever inseparable. They develop a feeling of obligation in the inheritors of our reality, supporting a tradition of preservation for the ages.

9. **A Living Obligation to an Economical Future**
Despite exceptional natural difficulties, the Seven Marvels of Conservation address a living obligation to an economical future. They are encouraging signs, showing us that it is feasible to beat misfortune, safeguard our planet, and secure a heritage for a long time into the future. They call upon us to act with earnestness and assurance.

10. **A Call to Embrace Our Obligation**

As we examine the getting through significance of these miracles, we should perceive that they are not simply far off images but rather living tokens of our obligation. Our activities today will shape the destiny of these contemplates and decide if they will proceed to motivate and improve the world for centuries to come.

All things being equal, the Seven Marvels of Conservation — UNESCO's Reality Legacy program — are not relics of the past; they are reference points directing us toward a maintainable, comprehensive, and agreeable future. They represent our common obligation to protecting the tradition of mankind and the planet. They challenge us to embrace our obligation as stewards of culture and nature. In their persevering through importance, we track down motivation, trust, and a significant feeling of direction — a reason that rises above ages and joins us in the respectable undertaking of protection.

Printed in the USA
CPSIA information can be obtained
at www.ICGtesting.com
LVHW021203201023
761658LV00050B/577